# Quick & Easy
# DEHYDRATED
# Meals in a Bag

# Quick & Easy DEHYDRATED Meals in a Bag

**Tammy Gangloff, Steven Gangloff, MD, and September Ferguson**

Stackpole Books
Guilford, CT

Published by Stackpole Books
An imprint of Globe Pequot
Trade Division of The Rowman & Littlefield Publishing Group, Inc.
4501 Forbes Boulevard, Suite 200, Lanham, Maryland 20706
www.rowman.com

Distributed by NATIONAL BOOK NETWORK

Photos by KC Kratt Photography

British Library Cataloguing in Publication Information Available

Library of Congress Cataloging-in-Publication Data
Names: Gangloff, Tammy, author. | Gangloff, Steven, author. | Ferguson,
   September, author.
Title: Quick & easy dehydrated meals in a bag / Tammy Gangloff, Steven
   Gangloff, and September Ferguson.
Other titles: Dehydrated meals in a bag | Quick and easy dehydrated meals
in a bag
Description: Guilford, CT : Stackpole Books, [2018] | Includes index.
Identifiers: LCCN 2017034440 (print) | LCCN 2017035712 (ebook) |
   ISBN 9780811766111 | ISBN 9780811719803 (pbk.) | ISBN
   9780811766111 (e-book)
Subjects: LCSH: Dried foods. | Food—Drying. | Lunchbox cooking. | LCGFT:
   Cookbooks.
Classification: LCC TX609 (ebook) | LCC TX609 .G348 2018 (print) | DDC
   641.4/4—dc23
LC record available at https://lccn.loc.gov/2017034440

♾™ The paper used in this publication meets the minimum requirements of
American National Standard for Information Sciences—Permanence of Paper
for Printed Library Materials, ANSI/NISO Z39.48-1992.

Printed in the United States of America

# Contents

# Dedication

I would like to dedicate this book to all the people who have written to us and posted requests and encouragement to compose a book specifically on packing meals in a bag. It was your loving support of our work in dehydrating that has made this book possible. I cannot thank you enough for all the love and kind words.

Special thanks—

To my amazing hard-working children who are also my coauthors, September Ferguson and Dr. Steven Gangloff.

To my loving and kind son Scott Gangloff and my son-in-law Steve Ferguson, thank you for all of your support.

To my incredibly sweet and adorable grandchildren Kaylee, Brayden, Parker, and Finn . . . I love you!

To our publisher.

To KC Kratt Photography.

To Kevin Telaak of Artisan Kitchen and Bath for allowing us to use one of his beautiful kitchens (cover photo).

—Tammy

# Chapter 1

# What Is a Meal in a Bag?

## INTRODUCTION

We've all done it: paid for the easy accessibility of store-bought meals in a box. You know what we're talking about! Walk down any grocery aisle and you will find boxes of easy meals or side dishes. The main work has been done, all the seasonings and spices are there; just add a few ingredients and you're ready in minutes.

Whether you're a stay-at-home mom or dad, a working parent, or a caregiver of any kind, life is crazy busy. We get it! We spend much of our lives running around between jobs, hobbies, and errands, shuttling the kids from place to place, all the while harboring that nagging question in the backs of our minds: "What am I making for dinner tonight?"

Often, we make what is fast and easy. But for this, we have to compromise. We pay extra money to purchase the pre-boxed meal, and we pay the health cost on these often over-processed and sodium-saturated items.

It's about time we share with you our secret to making easy, healthy, and cost-effective meals in a snap, using your own ingredients, *ready* at your fingertips. Don't fall out of your chair yet—we're just getting to the good part!

Our first book, *The Ultimate Dehydrator Cookbook*, showed you the art of food dehydration, preparation, and rehydration. We got you started with instructions on dehydrating foods from A to Z, and introduced you to rehydrating and making meals, desserts, and treats. In this book we will take you into a new realm of ingenuity as we tackle making "meals in a bag" with your dehydrated fruits and veggies.

Now, what exactly is a meal in a bag? It's the convenience of store-bought pre-prepared meals, without the compromise to your bank account and your health. It's the freedom to go beyond "Turkey Pieces and Gravy" and to create your own family-loved recipes; delicious, healthy, pre-prepared, pre-packaged, and ready to enjoy.

Why make meals in a bag? As hinted above, there are many benefits. A single-serving boxed meal will cost you a few dollars, or even close to ten dollars for a quality "lean" or "fit" version. Extrapolate that for your entire family, and you can see how much you are paying for convenience. With dehydrated foods you can purchase fresh items in bulk and in larger quantities, and store for years without the use of the electricity or the fear of freezer burn, and with less food waste. You can make a single bag meal containing the serving size needed for your whole family, saving on packaging cost and environmental impact. You will find your weekly grocery bill shrinking like a carrot in your dehydrator.

Important, too, are the health benefits of this venture. Try the "flip game" with your family next time you walk down your local grocer's frozen meal aisle. Try to guess the amount of preservatives in a meal, flip it over, and see if you were close. You will be shocked. A single one-cup serving of a popular brand of frozen lasagna contains 810 mg of sodium. Depending on your appetite, it is not hard to imagine consuming 1,620 to 2,430 mg of sodium in a single meal—even if you drink water and skip dessert. The FDA recommends that adults limit their sodium intake to *less* than 2,300 mg per *entire day*. A high-sodium diet is well recognized in the medical community as having a direct impact on blood pressure, a consequence that causes many long-term health problems.

This is just sodium. Imagine the other preservatives, calories, and saturated fats in these highly processed and flash-frozen items. Dehydration itself preserves the food, so any salt used in the recipes in this book is for taste and not preservation. Too, flash freezing is recognized by the Department of Agriculture to deplete vitamins and nutrients from food to a degree twenty to forty times that of dehydrating. When you make your meals yourself, you choose your own fresh ingredients. You know exactly what goes into what you feed your family. No more worrying about your family's allergies and dietary restrictions. No difficult-to-pronounce chemicals or additives. By doing it yourself, you have the ability to create a meal that is specific to your family's needs.

Custom-made meals in a bag are like having a whole grocery store at the tips of your fingers, and the best part is, it won't go bad! With our help, making meals in a bag is as simple as . . . well . . . apple pie in a bag!

## GETTING STARTED

Getting started is easy. Most of your meals in a bag will require the use of your already-dehydrated foods. If you have yet to dehydrate anything, then we suggest picking up *The Ultimate Dehydrator Cookbook*, our must-have A-to-Z guide for dehydrating. Also, some of the meals in this book will require fresh produce that we will teach you to dehydrate to make a complete meal, so get those dehydrators ready!

### Assembling Your Meals in a Bag

For optimal storage, your dehydrated items should be stored in vacuum-sealed bags containing an oxygen pack. Those vacuum-sealed bags may then be double-bagged inside a puncture-proof and light-proof Mylar bag, which you may label with the recipe title and instructions.

For the vacuum-bag ingredients, we have organized the recipes in this book into Large Bag and Small Bag categories, as sometimes certain items must be kept separate. Each bag should contain an oxygen pack and be vacuum-sealed separately.

We prefer to use fresh meat in our recipes, but if you choose to package freeze-dried meats with your meals it can be done, but meat must be placed inside a separate bag.

### Materials

**Dehydrator:** The dehydrator you choose is the most important part of the dehydrating process. If you do not have a good dehydrator it can really affect the efficiency with which you can dehydrate food. Check out *The Ultimate Dehydrator Cookbook* for an in-depth discussion of what to look for in a dehydrator. Here is a quick synopsis:

- Fan placement should be in the back of the dehydrator, not the top or bottom.
- Look for plastic mesh trays, as metal can burn your food.
- Temperature controls are a must! Different foods require different temperatures.
- Ditch the timer! You can't overdry your food, and the constant airflow will only benefit your food.

**Dehydrator Dryer Sheets:** These are not the mesh trays that come with the dehydrator but they are just as important. These are solid Teflon-coated 100 percent nonstick sheets that allow you to dry liquid or small items that could fall between the cracks of the mesh trays.

**Vacuum Sealer:** We suggest a heavy-duty vacuum sealer with dual (or double-piston) suction motors.

**Vacuum Bags:** The vacuum bags must be at least two-ply and three millimeters (mm) in thickness. We also recommend channeled (embossed, textured, or microchannel) bags because they contain grooves that allow for streamlined air removal, giving them a tighter seal. The bags are very important, so do not settle for a less-durable bag; it is what will keep your food safe.

**Mylar Bags:** These are also important to reflect heat and light away from the food, helping to increase the shelf life for long-term storage. For optimal storage, place your vacuum-sealed bags into a Mylar bag and then heat-seal the Mylar bag (you cannot vacuum seal a Mylar bag).

**Oxygen Packs:** These will remove any residual oxygen left around your food after vacuum-sealing, protecting your food from any degradation. A one-gallon bag will require one 100 cc pack.

**Desiccant Packs:** Similar to oxygen packs, desiccant packs are small packs designed to remove residual *water* from items. They may sometimes be called "clay packs" or "gel packs" based on the particular desiccant material. Properly dehydrated items should not require desiccant packs. However, if you do choose to use them, make sure they are food safe.

**Labels:** Labels are important. These should tell the name of the dish, the date it was dehydrated, and the cooking directions. You can write directly on your Mylar bag with a permanent marker if you wish. However, Mylar bags are reusable, so you may wish instead to use paper or sticker labels that can later be removed. You can even have fun with designing beautiful and fun labels! Think of how much nicer it will look when you gift a meal to a friend or family member with your own personal label design. "You eat with your eyes first," so let's make a great first impression!

## Bags and Sizes

Throughout our recipes, we have divided up our ingredients by bag size. We do this because some ingredients require a barrier between each other, or sometimes simply because they are used at different points throughout the recipe.

The medium and small bags can be translucent Ziploc freezer bags or vacuum-seal bags. Place these bags inside the large Mylar bag to separate food. Here is the breakdown:

Large Bag = 1-gallon Mylar bag
Medium Bag = 4 cups or 1 quart
Small Bag = 2 cups or 1 pint

**Oxygen Absorbers:**
50 cc for 1 quart and smaller
100 cc per 1 gallon

**Desiccant Packs (gel silica, activated carbon, or clay):**
1- to 2-gram packet per 1 quart
5-gram packet per 1 gallon
10-gram packet for 5 gallon

## Powdered Substitutions

# Powdered Dairy and Eggs

It is not safe or practical to attempt to dehydrate eggs, cheese, or milk with a home dehydrator. These items must be dehydrated with commercial equipment using special processes. For this reason, we use commercially-made powdered eggs, cheese, and milk in many of our recipes in order to give you a true meal-in-a-bag experience. You can find these items from trusted distributors online or in some stores.

However, if you do not wish to use powdered dairy and eggs, you can use fresh milk, eggs, and cheese from your refrigerator during the cooking process just before eating. Use the following to make approximate adjustments using fresh eggs, milk, and cheese:

**2 tablespoons powdered egg + 2½ tablespoons water ≈ 1 fresh egg**
**3 tablespoons powdered milk + 1 cup water ≈ 1 cup fresh milk**
**3 tablespoons powdered cheese + 1 cup water ≈ 1 cup shredded cheese, melted**

# Vinegar Powder

It is easy to powder your own vinegar, allowing you to use it in your sauces and spices. It is also great to mix with salt to make your own salt-and-vinegar seasoning for chips, fries, popcorn, and much more.

*Ingredients*

**8 cups white vinegar**
**½ cup baking soda**

*Directions*

1. Place vinegar and baking soda into a large pot, stirring until dissolved.
2. Bring to a boil, then reduce to simmer. Do not cover.
3. Simmer until liquid has evaporated to about one half the amount.
4. Pour remaining liquid into a glass 10 x 10-inch casserole dish.
5. Place in dehydrator at 135°F for 14 to 16 hours until an entirely dry, white clumpy powder forms.
6. Blend with blender to a smooth powder.
7. Store in a mason jar with oxygen pack, optional desiccant pack, and lid.

# Soy Sauce Powder

Homemade soy sauce powder can really open up the possibilities in your kitchen.

*Ingredients*

> 2 cups soy sauce
> 1 tablespoon cornstarch

*Directions*

1. Place soy sauce and cornstarch into a pot and bring to a boil, continuously stirring until thickened.
2. Pour into a small glass bowl and place in dehydrator at 135°F for 8 to 12 hours or until completely dry and powdered.
3. Store in a mason jar with oxygen pack, optional desiccant pack, and lid.

# Tomato Paste Powder

Making your own tomato paste powder can be a real time saver. Plus, think of the space you can save storing it in its lightweight powder form.

*Ingredients*

> 1 (6-ounce) can tomato paste
> 1 cup warm water

*Directions*

1. Blend ingredients together well until smooth (consistency of a thin pancake batter).
2. Pour onto dehydrator sheet and place in dehydrator at 125°F for 8 to 12 hours, or until completely dry and brittle.
3. Powder using a blender or by hand.
4. Store in a mason jar with oxygen pack, optional desiccant pack, and lid.

# Dehydrated Caramelized Onion Powder

Use this powder to add sweetness to your spices!

## Ingredients

   2 cups chopped fresh onions
   ½ cup water

## Directions

1. Using water only (do not use oil or cooking spray), fry chopped onions in a non-stick frying pan on high heat, continuously stirring with a rubber spatula until golden brown and translucent.
2. Place caramelized onions onto a dehydrator sheet and dehydrate at 135°F for 8 to 12 hours or until completely dried and crisp.
3. Powder using a mortar and pestle, stone grinder, or blender.
4. Store in a mason jar with oxygen pack, optional desiccant pack, and lid.

# Chapter 2

# Storing Your Meals

## ENEMIES OF LONG-TERM STORAGE

We already talked about the items you will need to begin storing your meals, but it is also important to quickly review the "Enemies of Long-Term Storage." If you have *The Ultimate Dehydrator Cookbook* or are familiar with our site Dehydrate2Store.com, then you probably know these by heart. However, if you are new to us, then it is very important that you know these rules to ensure longevity in your food storage. So, let's review.

If your food has been properly dehydrated, it can last for years! However, the way you store your food after dehydrating is just as important. There are six environmental enemies to food storage. If you can eliminate them or minimize your food's exposure, you will maximize the shelf life.

**1. Moisture:** Moisture allows for growth of mold and bacteria! So for that reason, you want to make sure your food is thoroughly dehydrated (95 percent or more of the moisture removed). While there is no way to accurately measure the exact amount of moisture that has been removed, we can rely on the visual, touch, and sound tests.

- Visual: no sign of moisture
- Touch: feels dry, not sticky or tacky; breaks, crumbles, or tears; higher-sugar items will be bendable but will not tear and do not clump together when squeezed
- Sound: most items should have a snap or crumble when broken, tear like paper, or make a clicking noise when dropped.

If you are still uncertain, always remember: "When in Doubt, Keep Drying It Out!" You can never over dry your food!

**2. Heat:** Exposure to heat can destroy many of the nutrients in your food. Even the slightest elevation in temperature can be harmful. It is always best to store your food in a cool, dry place.

**3. Oxygen:** Oxidation, over time, can degrade the nutrients in your food. By minimizing your food's exposure to oxygen you can increase its shelf life. Minimize oxidation by vacuum-sealing and using oxygen packs.

**4. Microorganisms:** Bacteria, mold, and fungi can be harmful to the human body and can also contribute to food degradation. Keep microorganisms at bay by practicing sanitary kitchen techniques and removing all moisture from your food before storing.

**5. Light:** Exposure to light can greatly impact the nutritional value and appearance of your food in a short period of time. Using Mylar bags can be an effective way to block light.

**6. Pests:** Rodents, insects, and maybe even your family pet are attracted to those yummy bags of food. Use good-quality heavy-duty plastic bags, buckets, and Mylar bags to keep those uninvited guests out of your food storage.

## SHELF LIFE

If stored properly, most dehydrated meals can be good for fifteen to thirty years. A meal in a bag can vary in its shelf life depending on what ingredients are used. For instance, baking powder can only be stored for a year before it loses its ability to activate, therefore bringing its shelf life down to one year. Commercially dehydrated dairy and freeze-dried meat products may also have a shorter shelf life, usually five to ten years for commercially dehydrated dairy and twenty-five-plus years for freeze-dried meats. Check your commercially dehydrated or freeze-dried products for their recommended shelf life.

# Chapter 3

# No-Boil Noodles and Spiraling

Before we dive into making meals in a bag, let's first introduce some dehydrated items that we will be making and using in our recipes. You will see these unique items, including no-boil noodles and spiraled fruits and veggies, in some of our recipes throughout this book. We taught you how to create the remaining dehydrated ingredients needed in this book in our last book, *The Ultimate Dehydrator Cookbook*, so keep it handy as a reference!

## NO-BOIL (INSTANT) NOODLES

Store-bought no-boil (or "instant") noodles are simply noodles that have been cooked in a factory and then dehydrated. With a dehydrator, you can do this at home for less cost, and with more freedom of creativity. Why pay a premium when you can make them yourself?

Not all recipes require no-boil noodles because some offer enough boiling liquid for the noodles to hydrate during preparation. However, casseroles and baked dishes do require a no-boil noodle. Is it necessary to boil noodles first? No, not really. Many people add extra liquid to their pasta dishes and bake them and have no issue with the consistency of the noodle. However, some people feel the consistency of the noodle is not the same without boiling. The noodle may seem gummy and tough if it is not boiled first. It all comes down to preference. We are going to instruct you on how to make a no-boil noodle using premade pasta, but please feel free to use homemade pasta if preferred. However, if our recipe calls for no-boil noodles and you do not wish to use them, just remember to increase your liquid so that there is enough to properly hydrate the noodles.

### Directions

1. Cook pasta per instructions on packaging, or hand-make and cook your own noodles.
2. Dehydrate at 135°F for 8 to 14 hours (depending on pasta size) until brittle and translucent.
3. Store with an oxygen pack in a vacuum bag, Mylar bag, or mason jar. Desiccant packs are optional. Avoid vacuum-sealing long noodles such as spaghetti, as they will break.

## Fun Tip

To create small no-boil lasagna noodles perfect for soups and skillets, cook large lasagna noodles until they are soft enough to cut easily into thirds. Then dehydrate, as above.

## SPIRALIZED FRUITS AND VEGETABLES

Spiraling, or spiralizing, fruits and veggies has become increasingly popular. When you spiralize, you cut an item into thin ribbon-like strips, effectively creating a vegetable or fruit "pasta." You may be most familiar with zucchini noodles (or "zoodles"), which are simply spiralized zucchini!

Spiralized vegetables are higher in nutrients and lower in refined carbohydrates compared to traditional pastas, and thus can be used as a healthier and more colorful alternative, while also providing a subtle, unique flavor twist. They can also be used as a garnish to your favorite dish, as a component to a fresh salad, and more!

Here are some other great items to spiralize: carrots, bell peppers, parsnips, cucumbers, plantains, butternut squash, beets, sweet potatoes, apples, and pears.

Here we will show you how to spiralize and how to create fun and easy-to-store dehydrated "bird's nests" with those spiraled items.

## Step 1: Spiralize

A spiralizer is a small and affordable kitchen appliance that will spiralize your fruits and veggies. There are numerous brands, shapes, and sizes of spiralizers, which range in price. They function similarly to a table-mounted apple peeler: you insert your item, spin the lever, and out comes your spiralized product. This appliance will greatly decrease your kitchen prep time.

Using a spiralizer is certainly the easiest way to go, but if you do not own and do not wish to purchase one, here are some great "life hacks" to do the trick!

1. Try a potato or julienne peeler: Though more time consuming, you can use a handheld peeler to delicately spiral firm items like zucchini and carrots. A julienne peeler, which is a potato peeler with a serrated edge to produce strips, is the better of the two options and yields a nicer product. It may be difficult to keep your ribbons at a constant width, but you will improve with practice.
2. Use a knife: Long items such as zucchini, cucumber, and bell peppers can be spiraled using a sharp knife and julienning technique. Make sure to make your matchstick cuts as long and uniform as possible!
3. Mandolin slicer: Very carefully, use a mandolin slicer to make long, wide pieces that can then be sliced to size with a knife.

All fruits and vegetables should be raw when spiralized, except beets. Beets should be cooked first in order to more easily peel and spiralize.

### Pro Tip

If you are having trouble getting nice uniform and firm ribbons, try placing your fruit or vegetable in the freezer for a few minutes.

## Step 2: Blanch

After spiraling, all vegetables need to be blanched. To blanch, simply place in boiling water for approximately 10 seconds, then remove. Fruits do not require blanching before dehydrating. Beets also do not require blanching because, as mentioned above, they were cooked before spiralizing.

## Step 3: Measure

After spiraling and possibly blanching your fruit or veggie, you will want to measure your final product. It is easiest to measure and store these items in one-cup portions. To measure, simply use a fork to twirl the item like spaghetti into a "bird's nest" measuring about one cup. Making your bird's nests uniform one-cup sizes makes for easy measuring in recipes later. The bird's nest bundles are also ideal for storage, as long noodles will become brittle and break when dehydrated, while the nests remain secure and intact. The purpose of the bird's nest is not to create a "bird's nest" as a finished product but instead to protect the spiraled vegetables from become crushed and crumbled during the storage process.

## Step 4 : Dehydrate

First, spray all fruits and some vegetables with lemon juice or ascorbic acid prior to dehydrating to preserve vibrant color. This should not alter the taste of your final product. Leafy green vegetables such as cabbage do not require lemon juice.

Line your dehydrator trays with your one-cup bird's nest bundles and dehydrate at 125°F until completely dry and brittle. Dehydration times may vary depending on the item being dehydrated. Roughly, this should take between 8 and 12 hours.

## Step 5: Create!

Use your premeasured spiralized bird's nests to make easy and fun recipes of all kinds! You will find spiralized bird's nest "noodles" used in some of the recipes in this book!

# Chapter 4

# Seasonings

Sure, you can purchase premade seasoning packets from your grocer, but why waste the money? Store-bought seasoning can cost as much as $15 or more for a small jar. Not to mention, you are stifling the fun and creativity of making your own. In this chapter you will learn to create your own convenient seasoning packs for just pennies, using your own ingredients.

By making these seasonings ahead of time you will cut down on much work down the road. A lot of our recipes in this book use these wonderful seasonings in order to reduce your prep time to seconds.

## Citrus & Dill Seasoning

A fresh and light seasoning. Great to use on chicken and seafood.

*Makes ½ cup*

*Ingredients*

    2 teaspoons onion powder
    2 teaspoons garlic powder
    ¼ cup powdered dehydrated lemon zest
    ¼ cup dehydrated dill

*Directions*

Combine ingredients in a bowl, mix to a coarse powder, then store in a spice jar.

## Taco Seasoning

Make your own for just a fraction of the store cost.

*Makes ⅔ cup*

*Ingredients*

    4 tablespoons chili powder
    1 teaspoon garlic powder
    1 teaspoon onion powder
    2 teaspoons paprika
    1 teaspoon red pepper flakes
    1⅓ tablespoon salt
    1⅓ tablespoon black pepper
    2 tablespoons ground cumin
    1 teaspoon crushed dehydrated oregano

*Directions*

Combine ingredients in a bowl, mix to a fine powder, then store in a spice jar.

# Spicy Roasted Red Pepper Seasoning

Add a new flair to everyday meals with this simple seasoning. Use in pastas, chicken, seafood, meatloaf, mac and cheese, eggs, and potatoes.

*Makes ⅔ cup*

*Ingredients*

- 4 tablespoons coarsely ground dehydrated roasted red bell peppers
- 2 tablespoons onion powder
- 2 teaspoons garlic powder
- 2 teaspoons salt
- ¼ teaspoon cayenne pepper
- 2 tablespoons coarsely ground dehydrated carrots
- 1 teaspoon dehydrated thyme
- 2 teaspoons dehydrated basil

*Directions*

Combine ingredients in a bowl, mix to a coarse powder, then store in a spice jar.

## Fun Tip

For a fun spicy mayo, combine 1 teaspoon Spicy Roasted Red Pepper Seasoning with ⅓ cup mayonnaise!

# Basil Pesto Seasoning

Use this as a seasoning for chicken or seafood, or make into Basil Pesto Dip (see page 29).

*Makes 1½ cups*

### Ingredients

- 1 teaspoon onion powder
- 1 teaspoon garlic powder
- 2 tablespoons dehydrated chopped sun-dried tomatoes
- 1 cup dehydrated basil
- 1 teaspoon dehydrated parsley
- ¼ cup pine nuts, coarsely ground
- 2 teaspoons dehydrated lemon zest

### Fun Tip

For delicious basil pesto mayo, combine 1 teaspoon Basil Pesto Seasoning with ⅓ cup mayonnaise!

### Directions

Combine ingredients in a bowl, grind to a coarse powder (a mortar and pestle works well), then store in a spice jar.

# BBQ Seasoning

Sprinkle on chicken or steak, fold into hamburger, or top baked beans.

*Makes 1 cup*

### Ingredients

- ½ cup brown sugar
- 1 tablespoon onion powder
- 1 tablespoon garlic powder
- 1 tablespoon paprika
- 1 tablespoon chili powder
- 1 tablespoon salt
- 1 tablespoon black pepper
- 1 teaspoon ground mustard
- 1 teaspoon cayenne pepper (optional)

### Directions

Combine ingredients in a bowl, mix to a fine powder, then store in a spice jar.

# Italian Seasoning

Use with chicken or seafood, add to meatballs, or make into a marinade or dressing. See below.

*Makes ⅔ cup*

*Ingredients*

  3 tablespoons dehydrated basil
  3 tablespoons dehydrated oregano
  3 tablespoons dehydrated parsley
  1 tablespoon garlic powder
  1 teaspoon onion powder
  1 teaspoon dehydrated thyme
  1 teaspoon dehydrated rosemary
  ¼ teaspoon black pepper

**Fun Tip**

For Italian dressing, add 2 tablespoons Italian Seasoning to ¼ cup white vinegar, ⅔ cup canola oil, and 2 tablespoons water. Whisk together. Makes 16 servings.

*Directions*

Combine ingredients in a bowl, mix to a coarse powder, then store in a spice jar.

**Fun Tip**

For Italian garlic bread, whisk 1 tablespoon Italian Seasoning into 1 stick of softened butter. Spread on bread, and sprinkle with Parmesan cheese. Place in oven at 400°F until bread is crisped and butter is melted, approximately 15 to 20 minutes.

# Spicy Buffalo Seasoning

A little goes a long way with this spice. Add to chicken, seafood, and even mayonnaise.

*Makes ¼ cup*

### Ingredients

> 1 tablespoon garlic powder
> 1 tablespoon onion powder
> ½ teaspoon Vinegar Powder (see page 6)
> 2 teaspoons cayenne pepper powder
> 2 teaspoons chili powder
> 2 teaspoons paprika
> ½ teaspoon powdered dehydrated lemon zest
> ½ teaspoon salt
> ½ teaspoon black pepper

## Fun Tip

For kickin' spicy Buffalo mayo, combine ½ teaspoon Spicy Buffalo Seasoning with ⅓ cup mayonnaise!

### Directions

Combine ingredients in a bowl, mix to a fine powder, then store in a spice jar.

# Spinach & Dill Seasoning

Great on chicken, in pasta, or as a dip.

*Makes 1¼ cups*

### Ingredients

> 1 cup crushed dehydrated spinach
> 2 tablespoons dehydrated minced green onions
> 1 tablespoon dehydrated dill
> 1 teaspoon garlic powder
> 1 teaspoon onion powder
> 1 teaspoon dehydrated lemon zest

### Directions

Combine ingredients in a bowl, mix to a coarse powder, then store in a spice jar.

# Sweet Caramelized Onion Seasoning

Add to chicken, soups, pastas, meats, or seafood.

*Makes 1 cup*

### Ingredients

½ cup Caramelized Onion Powder (see page 8)
1 tablespoon mustard powder
1 tablespoon poppy seeds
¼ cup dehydrated red bell peppers, powdered
2 tablespoons garlic powder

### Directions

Combine ingredients in a bowl, grind to a coarse powder (a mortar and pestle works well), then store in a spice jar.

## Fun Tip

For Sweet Caramelized Onion dressing, add 2 tablespoons seasoning to ¼ cup white vinegar, ⅔ cup canola oil, and 2 tablespoons water. Whisk together. Makes 16 servings.

# Jamaican Jerk Seasoning

Sprinkle on meats or vegetables to give them an extra little kick.

*Makes about 1¼ cups*

### Ingredients

½ cup onion powder
¼ cup sea salt
¼ cup thyme
2 tablespoons cinnamon
1 tablespoon allspice
2 teaspoons cayenne pepper

### Directions

Combine ingredients in a bowl, mix to a fine powder, then store in a spice jar.

# Ranch Seasoning

This seasoning is great on just about anything you can think of: meats, potatoes, and even mac and cheese!

*Makes about 1 cup*

### Ingredients

⅓ cup buttermilk powder
2 tablespoons dehydrated parsley
2 tablespoons dehydrated dill
2 teaspoons garlic powder
2 teaspoons onion powder
2 teaspoons dehydrated minced onion
2 teaspoons dehydrated minced chives
1 teaspoon black pepper
1 teaspoon salt

## Fun Tip

To make ranch dressing, combine 3 tablespoons Ranch Seasoning, 1 cup milk, and 1 cup mayonnaise. Blend and store in the refrigerator. Makes 2 cups.

### Directions

Combine ingredients in a bowl, mix to a coarse powder, then store in a spice jar.

# Meatloaf Seasoning

Store this seasoning in individually sealed bags. Use each bag of seasoning with 1 pound of ground beef.

*Makes 1 bag of seasoning mix*

### Ingredients

1 teaspoon mustard powder
1 teaspoon paprika
½ teaspoon salt
¾ teaspoon dehydrated basil
½ teaspoon black pepper
1 teaspoon garlic powder
1 teaspoon onion powder

*Directions*

Combine ingredients in a bowl, mix to a coarse powder, then store in individual small bags.

# Pumpkin Pie Spice

This staple spice can be used for so much more than just pie! Try it in baked goods, coffees, lattes, yogurt, and much more.

*Makes ½ cup*

*Ingredients*

> 4 tablespoons cinnamon
> 2 tablespoons coarsely ground dehydrated ginger
> 2 teaspoons allspice
> 2 teaspoons ground cloves
> 2 teaspoons ground mace
> 2 teaspoons ground nutmeg

*Directions*

Combine ingredients in a bowl, mix to a coarse powder, then store in a spice jar.

# Sweet Asian Spice

Great for stir-fry or on beef, chicken, or seafood.

*Makes about ⅔ cup*

## Ingredients

> 4 tablespoons sesame seeds
> 2 tablespoons powdered dehydrated ginger
> 2 tablespoons dehydrated toasted coconut
> 2 teaspoons garlic powder
> 1 teaspoon powdered dehydrated chile peppers
> 2 teaspoons sugar
> 2 teaspoons Soy Sauce Powder (see page 7)

## Directions

Combine ingredients in a bowl, mix to a coarse powder, then store in a spice jar.

# Italian Breadcrumbs

Perfect for coating chicken, fish, or pork, or as a perfect topping for any casserole dish.

*Makes 2 cups*

## Ingredients

> 2 cups dehydrated breadcrumbs
> 1 tablespoon Italian Seasoning (see page 19)

## Directions

Place ingredients in a blender and mix to a coarse powder. Pour into a small or medium vacuum-sealer bag, and vacuum-seal with an oxygen pack.

# Savory Sage and Onion Breadcrumbs

Add a little extra kick to any meal. Use to coat fish, chicken, or pork, or as a topping on casserole or mac and cheese.

*Makes 2 cups*

*Ingredients*

> 2 cups dehydrated breadcrumbs
> 1 tablespoon crushed dehydrated parsley
> 1 teaspoon sea salt
> 1 teaspoon black pepper
> ¼ teaspoon crushed dehydrated sage
> ¼ teaspoon onion powder
> ¼ teaspoon garlic powder
> ⅛ teaspoon powdered dehydrated cayenne pepper

*Directions*

Place ingredients in a blender and mix to coarse powder. Pour into a small or medium vacuum-sealer bag, and vacuum-seal with an oxygen pack.

# Lemon and Mint Breadcrumbs

This breadcrumb recipe is perfect for coating seafood or lamb. Also try it in stuffed mushrooms!

*Makes 2 cups*

*Ingredients*

> 2 cups dehydrated breadcrumbs
> 1 teaspoon dehydrated lemon zest
> 1 tablespoon crushed dehydrated mint leaves

*Directions*

Place ingredients in a blender and mix to coarse powder. Pour into a small or medium vacuum-sealer bag, and vacuum-seal with an oxygen pack.

# Chile and Lime Breadcrumbs

Try this on chicken fingers or your next Mexican-inspired casserole dish.

*Makes 2 cups*

### Ingredients

- 2 cups dehydrated breadcrumbs
- 2 dehydrated whole poblano peppers, coarsely ground
- 1 teaspoon dehydrated lime zest
- ½ teaspoon garlic powder
- ½ teaspoon sea salt

### Directions

Place ingredients in a blender and mix to a coarse powder. Pour into a small or medium vacuum-sealer bag, and vacuum-seal with an oxygen pack.

# Chapter 5

# Appetizers and Dips

Appetizers and dips are essentials, whether for the Super Bowl party, a baby shower, or just a movie night at home. Don't waste time that you could spend partying! Instead, try these fast and easy recipes made with just a few ingredients and your own premade seasonings at your next big get-together.

# Caramelized Onion, Squash, and Goat Cheese Turnovers

Wow your guests with this easy creamy appetizer!

*Makes 8 servings*

## Ingredients

¼ cup dehydrated squash, finely ground
1½ cups boiling water
1 tablespoon Sweet Onion Seasoning (see page 21)
½ cup goat cheese
1 can prepared croissant dough

## Directions

1. Preheat oven to 350°F.
2. Place dehydrated squash into a bowl and pour boiling water over it. Cover and set aside for 20 minutes.
3. Add seasoning, and fold in goat cheese.
4. Arrange croissant dough on a nonstick baking sheet. In the center of each croissant, place a dollop of the mixture, then fold edges over.
5. Bake for 20 minutes.

# Creamy Horseradish and Lemon Dill Dip

This dip pairs well with both veggies and potato chips.

*Makes 1½ cups*

## Ingredients

8 ounces cream cheese, softened
¼ cup sour cream
¼ cup horseradish
2 tablespoons Citrus & Dill Seasoning (see page 16)

*Directions*

1. Mix all ingredients together in a bowl until well blended, then chill in refrigerator for 30 minutes.
2. Serve with cold, crisp veggies or potato chips.

# Basil Pesto Dip

Dip it, try it in pasta, or spread it on your next sandwich; you won't be disappointed!

*Makes 8 servings*

*Ingredients*

> 2 tablespoons Basil Pesto Seasoning (see page 18)
> 2 tablespoons water
> 1½ tablespoons extra-virgin olive oil
> 1 tablespoon Parmesan cheese

*Directions*

1. Combine all ingredients in a bowl.
2. Spread on bread, crostini or mozzarella, or simply add to pasta or rice. (See Basil Pesto Rice on page 66.)

# Cold & Sweet Onion Dip

Whip this up in just minutes.

*Makes 6 servings*

*Ingredients*

> 1 tablespoon Sweet Caramelized Onion Seasoning (see page 21)
> 1 cup sour cream
> 2 ounces cream cheese, softened

*Directions*

1. Mix ingredients together in a bowl and chill in refrigerator for 30 minutes.
2. Serve with cool, crisp veggies.

# Hot & Creamy Sweet Onion Dip

This hot and creamy dip will have everyone coming back for more.

*Makes 10–12 servings*

### Ingredients

1 tablespoon Sweet Caramelized Onion Seasoning (see page 21)
8 ounces cream cheese, softened
1 cup mayonnaise
1 cup Parmesan cheese

### Directions

1. Preheat oven to 350°F.
2. Mix all ingredients in a bowl, then transfer to a small casserole dish.
3. Bake uncovered at 350°F for 45 minutes or until the top is bubbly and lightly browned.
4. Serve with chunks of bread or crostini for dipping.

# Spinach and Dill Dip

It is hard to decide which is more surprising: how good it tastes or how easy it was to make!

### Ingredients

1 tablespoon Spinach & Dill Seasoning (see page 20)
½ cup sour cream
¼ cup mayonnaise

### Directions

1. Mix ingredients together in a bowl and chill in refrigerator for 30 minutes.
2. Serve with cool, crisp veggies or chunks of bread.

# Spicy Mexican Bean Dip

This spicy dip is a real crowd-pleaser. Try dressing it up with a dollop of sour cream!

*Serves 8*

## Large Bag

   1 cup dehydrated refried beans, crumbled
   1 tablespoon Taco Seasoning (see page 16)
   1 tablespoon dehydrated diced tomatoes
   ¼ teaspoon crushed dehydrated jalapeños
   2 teaspoons dehydrated chopped onions
   ½ teaspoon finely ground dehydrated lime zest

## To Store

In a blender, combine dehydrated ingredients and blend until smooth.

   Place in a canning jar, or vacuum-seal with an oxygen pack and double-bag in Mylar for long-term storage.

## Cooking Ingredients

   1⅓ cup boiling water
   ¼ cup shredded Mexican cheese

## To Rehydrate

1. Open storage bag and pour contents into a small oven-safe bowl, then add boiling water. Stir, cover, and let sit for 20 minutes to rehydrate.
2. Stir again, cover, and place in refrigerator for 30 minutes.
3. Preheat oven to 350°F.
4. Sprinkle shredded cheese on top of dip and bake for 20 to 30 minutes.
5. Remove and serve hot with tortilla chips.

# Summertime Lemon & Mint Hummus

This refreshing hummus can be made first and then dehydrated and stored, for a fast appetizer in a snap!

*Makes 2½ cups*

### Large Bag

> 1 cup dehydrated pureed chickpeas, crumbled
> 3 tablespoons sesame seeds
> 1 tablespoon onion powder
> ½ teaspoon garlic powder
> 3 tablespoons crushed dehydrated mint leaves
> 2 tablespoons crushed dehydrated parsley
> 1 teaspoon powdered dehydrated lemon zest
> 1½ teaspoons sea salt

### To Store

In a blender, combine dehydrated ingredients and blend until smooth. Place in a canning jar, or vacuum-seal with an oxygen pack and double-bag in Mylar for long-term storage.

### Cooking Ingredients

> 2½ cups boiling water
> ¼ cup extra-virgin olive oil

### To Rehydrate

1. Open dehydrated hummus bag and pour into a small heat-safe bowl, then add boiling water.
2. Let sit for 2 to 3 minutes, then stir, cover, and refrigerate for 2 hours. It will thicken as it chills.
3. Stir in extra-virgin olive oil before serving.

# Spicy Roasted Red Pepper Hummus

This hummus is a great balance between spicy and sweet. It can be made first and then dehydrated for easy storage, for a fast and easy appetizer!

*Makes 2 cups*

### Large Bag

- 1 cup dehydrated pureed chickpeas, crumbled
- 3 tablespoons sesame seeds
- 1 tablespoon Spicy Roasted Red Pepper Seasoning (see page 17)

### To Store

In a blender, combine dehydrated ingredients and blend until smooth.

Place in a canning jar, or vacuum-seal with an oxygen pack and double-bag in Mylar for long-term storage.

### Cooking Ingredients

- 2 cups boiling water
- ¼ cup extra-virgin olive oil

### To Rehydrate

1. Open dehydrated hummus bag and pour into a small heat-safe bowl, then add boiling water.
2. Let sit for 2 to 3 minutes, then stir, cover, and refrigerate for 2 hours. It will thicken as it chills.
3. Stir in extra-virgin olive oil before serving.

# Sweet Caramelized Onion Hummus

This sweet and creamy hummus can be made first and then dehydrated for easy storage, for a quick appetizer.

*Makes 2 cups*

### Large Bag

    1 cup dehydrated pureed chickpeas, crumbled
    3 tablespoons sesame seeds
    1 tablespoon Sweet Caramelized Onion Seasoning (see page 21)

### To Store

In a blender, combine dehydrated ingredients and blend until smooth.

Place in a canning jar, or vacuum-seal with an oxygen pack and double-bag in Mylar for long-term storage.

### Cooking Ingredients

    2 cups boiling water
    ¼ cup extra-virgin olive oil

### To Rehydrate

1. Open dehydrated hummus bag and pour into a small heat-safe bowl, then add boiling water.
2. Let sit for 2 to 3 minutes, then stir, cover, and refrigerate for 2 hours. It will thicken as it chills.
3. Stir in extra-virgin olive oil before serving.

# Kale and Garlic Hummus

Kale is known as a "superfood" due to its high vitamin and antioxidant content. This recipe is not just great tasting, it's good for you! Win-win.

*Makes 2½ cups*

*Large Bag*

> 1 cup dehydrated pureed chickpeas, crumbled
> 3 tablespoons sesame seeds
> ½ teaspoon finely ground dehydrated garlic
> 1 cup dehydrated kale leaves
> ½ teaspoon dehydrated lemon zest
> ½ teaspoon sea salt

*To Store*

In a blender, combine dehydrated ingredients and blend until smooth.

Place in a canning jar, or vacuum-seal with an oxygen pack and double-bag in Mylar for long-term storage.

*Cooking Ingredients*

> 2½ cups boiling water
> ¼ cup extra-virgin olive oil

*To Rehydrate*

1. Open dehydrated hummus bag and pour into a small heat-safe bowl, then add boiling water.
2. Let sit for 2 to 3 minutes, then stir, cover, and refrigerate for 2 hours. It will thicken as it chills.
3. Stir in extra-virgin olive oil before serving.

# Citrus and Dill Cheese Ball

This is a great summertime dip, but we won't stop you from enjoying it year-round.

*Makes 1 baseball-sized cheese ball, or about 8 servings*

### Ingredients

2 tablespoons Citrus & Dill Seasoning (see page 16)
8 ounces cream cheese, softened
4 ounces shredded mild provolone cheese

### Directions

1. Mix all ingredients in a bowl, then place the mixture onto plastic wrap and roll into a ball.
2. Chill for 2 hours in the refrigerator, then serve with your favorite veggies or crackers.

# Chapter 6

# Pour-and-Go Meals

What if preparing dinner was actually the easiest part of your day? With "pour-and-go" slow-cooker and rice-cooker recipes, we take all the difficulty out of meal prep and use both your dehydrated foods and storage to their true potential. Pour-and-go meals are delicious custom meals prepared in advance by you using your dehydrated and other ingredients, and stored in vacuum bags for easy use when you need them. You can make numerous recipes in bulk at once, saving huge amounts of time in the future. These recipes last for many years without the need for potentially harmful chemical preservatives. Simply open a bag, pour in a slow cooker or rice cooker on the way out the door, and when you return home dinner is ready with just a few finishing touches. No hassle and easy cleanup. Your family will recognize you as a dinner rockstar each night. Don't worry, we won't tell them your secret!

# Clam Chowder

An easy slow-cooker soup with a delicate creamy texture and mild flavor. Try adding some crumbled bacon on top as seasoning!

*Serves 6*

### Large Bag

> 1 tablespoon dehydrated chopped onion
> 3 tablespoons dehydrated chopped celery
> 2 cups dehydrated chopped or sliced potatoes

### Small Bag

> ½ teaspoon thyme
> ¼ teaspoon ground pepper
> ¼ cup all-purpose flour

### To Store

Place all ingredients into bags. Place small bag into large bag, seal, and label with cooking instructions.

### Cooking Ingredients

> 6 cups water
> 12 ounces (canned) minced clams with juice
> 2 cups half-and-half

### Directions

1. Place ingredients from large and small bags into slow cooker.
2. Add water and minced clams with juice.
3. Cook on high heat for 4 to 5 hours or low for 7 to 8 hours.
4. Add the half-and-half, cover, and cook 30 more minutes. Enjoy!

# Lentil Soup

A hearty slow-cooker soup.

*Serves 6*

*Large Bag*

   ½ cup dry split mung beans
   ⅔ cup dry split lentils
   1 teaspoon ground turmeric
   ¼ teaspoon dried mustard seeds
   ¼ teaspoon dried fennel seeds
   1 teaspoon dehydrated lemon zest
   ½ teaspoon dehydrated hot cherry pepper, crushed

*Small Bag*

   ¼ cup dehydrated corn
   ½ cup dehydrated ½-inch cubed potatoes
   1 tablespoon dehydrated chopped onion

*To Store*

Place all ingredients into bags. Place small bag into large bag, seal, and label with cooking instructions.

*Cooking Ingredients*

   8 cups water

*Directions*

1. Place ingredients from large and small bags into slow cooker with water.
2. Cook on high heat for 5 to 6 hours or low for 8 to 9 hours.

# Beef and Cabbage Soup

A hearty soup that is loaded with healthy vegetables.

*Serves 8*

### Large Bag

>    4 cups dehydrated shredded cabbage
>    ½ cup dehydrated shredded carrots
>    ½ cup dehydrated shredded onions
>    ½ cup dehydrated sliced mushrooms

### Small Bag

>    4 teaspoons beef bouillon

### To Store

Place all ingredients into bags. Place small bag into large bag, seal, and label with cooking instructions.

### Cooking Ingredients

>    1 pound cooked ground beef

### Directions

1.  Place all ingredients from large and small bags into slow cooker with the water.
2.  Add the cooked ground beef.
3.  Cook on high heat for 4 to 5 hours or low for 7 to 8 hours.

# Pumpkin Pie Soup

This creamy soup tastes like dessert, but without the guilt.

*Serves 6*

### Large Bag

   ⅔ cup finely ground/powdered dehydrated pumpkin
   3 teaspoons chicken bouillon
   2 tablespoons Pumpkin Pie Spice (see page 23)
   2 tablespoons brown sugar

### To Store

Place all ingredients into large bag, seal, and label with cooking instructions.

### Cooking Ingredients

   8 cups water
   ½ cup half-and-half

### Directions

1.  Place ingredients from large bag into slow cooker, and add the water.
2.  Cook on high heat for 4 to 5 hours or low for 7 to 8 hours.
3.  Stir half-and-half into soup until well blended. Serve hot.

# Beef Stew

A hearty stew has never been so easy.

*Serves 8*

### Large Bag

½ cup dehydrated whole baby carrots

4 cups dehydrated sliced potatoes

2 cups dehydrated sliced mushrooms

1 cup dehydrated sliced onion

2 tablespoons dehydrated chopped celery

1 cup dehydrated chopped tomatoes

1 teaspoon dehydrated crushed garlic

### Small Bag

¼ cup all-purpose flour

1 tablespoon cornstarch

½ teaspoon dried thyme

1 tablespoon beef bouillon

### To Store

Place all ingredients into bags. Place small bag into large bag, seal, and label with cooking instructions.

### Cooking Ingredients

2 pounds raw stew beef, cubed

12 cups warm water

### Directions

1. Place meat into bottom of slow cooker.
2. Pour ingredients from large bag only over top of beef (do not stir).
3. Pour ingredients from small bag into a blender with warm water, and blend for 2 to 3 minutes.
4. Pour blended mixture atop the veggies and beef in the slow cooker (do not stir).
5. Cook, covered, on high heat for 6 hours or low 8 hours, stirring once hourly.

# Apple-Raisin Chicken Stew

A sweet and savory full-bodied stew.

*Serves 6*

*Large Bag*

>    2 cups dehydrated sliced apples
>    1 cup raisins
>    1 cup dehydrated sliced carrots
>    ¼ cup dehydrated sliced onion
>    2 tablespoon dehydrated parsley

*Small Bag*

>    1 teaspoon caraway seeds
>    1 teaspoon dried thyme
>    ¼ teaspoon Vinegar Powder (see page 6)
>    1 tablespoon brown sugar
>    1 tablespoon cornstarch

*To Store*

Place all ingredients into bags. Place small bag into large bag, seal, and label with cooking instructions.

*Cooking Ingredients*

>    1½ pounds chicken breasts, cubed
>    8½ cups warm water

*Directions*

1.  Sauté chicken in skillet for 4 to 5 minutes or until all sides are browned, then place into bottom of slow cooker.
2.  Pour ingredients from large bag only into slow cooker over chicken.
3.  Place ingredients from small bag into a blender with the warm water and blend until dissolved.
4.  Pour blended mixture over veggies and chicken.
5.  Cook on high heat for 4 to 5 hours or low for 7 to 8 hours.

# Spicy Pumpkin and Kale Stew

Kale is a superfood. Pumpkin is super good. You're a super chef. It was meant to be.

*Serves 8*

*Large Bag*

- ½ cup dry black beans
- ½ cup dry pinto beans
- ½ cup dry great northern beans
- ¼ cup powdered dehydrated pumpkin
- 1 teaspoon chili powder
- 1 teaspoon dried oregano
- 1 teaspoon salt
- 1½ teaspoons ground cumin
- 3 teaspoons chicken bouillon
- 1 teaspoon crushed dehydrated hot red pepper

*Medium Bag*

- 1 cup dehydrated sliced tomato
- ½ cup dehydrated sliced onions
- 3 cups dehydrated chopped kale

*To Store*

Place all ingredients into bags. Place medium bag into large bag, seal, and label with cooking instructions.

*Cooking Ingredients*

- 12 cups water

*Directions*

1. Place all ingredients from large bag and medium bag into slow cooker.
2. Add water.
3. Cook on high heat 7 to 8 hours.

# Beef, Barley, and Spinach Soup

A hearty soup great for those cold winter nights.

*Serves 8*

### Large Bag

½ cup dehydrated thinly sliced carrots

1 cup dehydrated sliced tomatoes

¼ cup dehydrated chopped onions

2 cups dehydrated baby spinach

⅔ cup cooking barley

### Small Bag

2 teaspoons beef bouillon

1½ teaspoons dehydrated thyme

1 teaspoon dehydrated oregano

½ teaspoon powdered dehydrated garlic

¼ teaspoon black pepper

### To Store

Place all ingredients into bags. Place small bag into large bag, seal, and label with cooking instructions.

### Cooking Ingredients

1 pound ground beef

8 cups water

### Directions

1. In a large skillet, brown ground beef.
2. Add all ingredients from large and small bags into slow cooker with water. Add cooked ground beef. Slow cook on high 6 to 7 hours.

# Mint Pea Soup

This refreshing soup can be served hot or cold.

*Serves 6*

### Large Bag

> 6 cups dried split peas
> 1 tablespoon dehydrated diced shallots
> ¼ cup dehydrated parsley
> ¼ cup dehydrated mint leaves
> 1 teaspoon powdered dehydrated lemon
> 2 teaspoons vegetable bouillon

### To Store

Place all ingredients into large bag, seal, and label with cooking instructions.

### Cooking Ingredients

> 10 cups boiling water
> ¼ cup heavy cream

### Directions

1. Place large bag into slow cooker with water, and whisk for 1 minute.
2. Cook on high heat 6 to 7 hours.
3. Whisk in heavy cream just prior to serving.

# Hawaiian Ham Casserole

Perfect for your Hawaiian theme party. This sweet and hearty dish will keep your guests coming back for more . . . we can't say the same about your ukulele playing.

*Serves 6*

*Large Bag*

> 2 cups uncooked white rice
> ¼ cup dehydrated sliced carrots
> ¼ cup dehydrated sliced green bell pepper
> ¼ cup dehydrated shredded onion

*Medium Bag*

> 1 cup dehydrated pineapple tidbits
> 1 cup raisins

*Small Bag*

> 3 tablespoons cornstarch
> 3 teaspoons ground mustard
> 1 teaspoon Vinegar Powder (see page 6)
> 1 teaspoon Soy Sauce Powder (see page 7)

*To Store*

Place all ingredients into bags. Place smaller bags into large bag, seal, and label with cooking instructions.

*Cooking Ingredients*

> 9 cups water
> 2 cups cubed cooked ham

*Directions*

1. Place ingredients from all three bags into slow cooker, along with water and ham.
2. Cook on high heat for 4 to 5 hours or low for 7 to 8 hours.

# Beef Taco and Potato Casserole

A slow-cooker casserole that is sure to please!

*Serves 6*

### Large Bag

    2 cups dehydrated sliced potatoes
    ¼ cup dehydrated shredded onion
    ¼ cup dehydrated corn
    1 cup dehydrated sliced tomatoes

### Small Bag

    2 tablespoons Taco Seasoning (see page 16)
    ½ cup powdered cheese
    3 tablespoons powdered nonfat milk

### To Store

Place all ingredients into bags. Place small bag into large bag, seal, and label with cooking instructions.

### Cooking Ingredients

    1 pound cooked ground beef
    9 cups water

### Directions

1. Add cooked ground beef to slow cooker.
2. Add ingredients from large and small bags to slow cooker, plus water.
3. Cook on high heat for 4 to 5 hours or low for 7 to 8 hours.

# Unstuffed Peppers

All the wonderful flavors of stuffed peppers in a quick and easy slow-cooker casserole.

*Serves 6*

*Large Bag*

> 2 cups uncooked rice

*Small Bag*

> 2 cups dehydrated sliced (½-inch strips) green bell peppers
> ¼ cup dehydrated shredded onion

*To Store*

Place all ingredients into bags. Place small bag into large bag, seal, and label with cooking instructions.

*Cooking Ingredients*

> 1 pound cooked ground beef
> 1 (26-ounce) jar marinara sauce
> 4 cups water

*Directions*

1. Place ingredients from large and small bags into slow cooker.
2. Add the cooked ground beef, marinara sauce, and water, and stir together.
3. Cook on high heat for 4 to 5 hours or low for 7 to 8 hours.

# Cabbage and Turkey Casserole

Healthier than beef cabbage rolls but with just as much flavor.

*Serves 6 to 8*

### Large Bag

    4 cups dehydrated shredded cabbage
    1 cup dehydrated shredded onion
    1 cup dehydrated sliced tomatoes
    ½ cup dehydrated corn

### Small Bag

    2 tablespoons Spicy Roasted Red Pepper Seasoning (see page 17)
    1 tablespoon powdered tomato paste
    2 teaspoons cornstarch

### To Store

Place all ingredients into bags. Place small bag into large bag, seal, and label with cooking instructions.

### Cooking Ingredients

    10 cups water
    1½ pounds cooked ground turkey

### Directions

1. Place ingredients in large and small bags into slow cooker.
2. Add water, stirring until blended and powders are dissolved, then add the cooked ground turkey.
3. Cook on high heat for 5 to 6 hours or low for 7 to 8 hours.

# Green Beans and Mushroom Casserole

Just add water and this classic side dish just got a whole lot easier.

*Serves 8*

*Large Bag*

> 2 cups dehydrated French cut green beans
> ½ cup dehydrated shredded onions
> 1 cup dehydrated sliced mushrooms

*Medium Bag*

> 1 cup Savory Sage and Onion Breadcrumbs (see page 25)

*Small Bag*

> 2 teaspoons beef bouillon
> 3 tablespoons flour
> 1 teaspoon crushed dehydrated garlic
> ¼ teaspoon ground pepper

*To Store*

Place all ingredients into bags. Place smaller bags into large bag, seal, and label with cooking instructions.

*Cooking Ingredients*

> 7 cups water

*Directions*

1. Place ingredients from large and small bags into a slow cooker. Reserve medium bag.
2. Add water, stirring until powder is blended and dissolved.
3. Cook on high heat for 5 to 6 hours or low for 7 to 8 hours.
4. Remove cover and sprinkle on the Savory Sage and Onion Breadcrumbs.
5. Replace cover and cook an additional hour.

# Sweet and Sour Chicken

Everyone's favorite takeout, now right out of your slow cooker.

*Serves 6*

*Large Bag*

>   1 cup dehydrated pineapple tidbits
>   1 cup dehydrated sliced carrots
>   ½ cup dehydrated sliced onions
>   ½ cup dehydrated sliced green bell pepper
>   ¼ cup dehydrated water chestnuts
>   ¼ cup dehydrated snow peas

*Small Bag*

>   1 teaspoon powdered dehydrated ginger
>   ½ teaspoon Soy Sauce Powder (see page 7)
>   ½ cup brown sugar
>   ½ teaspoon Vinegar Powder (see page 6)
>   2 teaspoons powdered dehydrated tomato paste
>   1 tablespoon cornstarch

*To Store*

Place all ingredients into bags. Place small bag into large bag, seal, and label with cooking instructions.

*Cooking Ingredients*

>   1½ pounds chicken, cut into strips
>   9 cups warm water

*Directions*

1. Sauté the sliced chicken in a skillet for 4 to 5 minutes, then placed into bottom of slow cooker.
2. Pour ingredients from large bag only into slow cooker over the chicken.
3. Pour ingredients from small bag into a blender with the warm water and blend for two minutes.
4. Pour the blended mixture into slow cooker and cover.
5. Cook on high heat for 5 to 6 hours or low for 7 to 8 hours.

# Sweet Pepper Chicken

Serve this easy chicken recipe on its own or over cooked rice.

*Serves 6*

*Large Bag*

> 1 cup dehydrated green bell pepper strips
> 1 cup dehydrated red bell pepper strips
> 1 cup dehydrated yellow bell pepper strips
> 1 cup dehydrated sliced mushrooms

*Small Bag*

> 3 tablespoons powdered nonfat milk
> 1 tablespoon cornstarch
> 1 tablespoon chicken bouillon
> 2 teaspoons Citrus & Dill Seasoning (see page 16)

*To Store*

Place all ingredients into bags. Place small bag into large bag, seal, and label with cooking instructions.

*Cooking Ingredients*

> 3 chicken breasts, cut into quarters
> 6 cups warm water

*Directions*

1. Sauté chicken in a skillet until brown on each side, then transfer to slow cooker.
2. Pour ingredients from large bag only over top of chicken.
3. Pour ingredients from small bag into blender with the warm water and blend until dissolved.
4. Pour blended mixture over veggies and chicken.
5. Cover and cook on high heat for 4 to 5 hours or low for 7 to 8 hours. Great served over cooked rice.

# Apple-Barley Chicken

The sweetness of apples pairs excellently with the robustness of curry and barley.

*Serves 6*

*Large Bag*

    1 cup dehydrated apple slices, cut in half
    ¼ cup dehydrated sliced onion
    ¼ cup dehydrated chopped red bell pepper
    ¼ cup dehydrated chopped green bell pepper

*Small Bag*

    1 tablespoon chicken bouillon
    1 tablespoon curry powder
    1 cup medium pearl barley

*To Store*

Place all ingredients into bags. Place small bag into large bag, seal, and label with cooking instructions.

*Cooking Ingredients*

    3 chicken breasts, cubed
    6 cups warm water

*Directions*

1. Sauté cubed chicken in skillet until all sides are brown, then place into slow cooker.
2. Pour ingredients from large and small bags into slow cooker over the chicken.
3. Stir in the warm water, then cover.
4. Cook on high heat for 4 to 5 hours or low for 7 to 8 hours.

# Cabbage Chili

Sweet cabbage brings a surprising twist to ordinary chili.

*Serves 6*

*Large Bag*

> 6 cups dehydrated shredded cabbage
> 2 cups dehydrated sliced tomatoes
> 1 cup dehydrated shredded onion
> 1 tablespoon dehydrated chopped green chiles
> 1 cup dry pinto beans

*Small Bag*

> 1 tablespoon Spicy Roasted Red Pepper Seasoning (see page 17)
> 1 teaspoon chili powder
> 1 tablespoon cornstarch

*To Store*

Place all ingredients into bags. Place small bag into large bag, seal, and label with cooking instructions.

*Cooking Ingredients*

> 1 pound cooked ground beef
> 12 cups warm water

*Directions*

1. Place ground beef into slow cooker.
2. Add ingredients from large and small bags into slow cooker
3. Add the warm water, stirring until powder is dissolved, and cover.
4. Cook on high heat for 4 to 5 hours or low for 7 to 8 hours.

# Thanksgiving Casserole

All the flavors of Thanksgiving in one easy slow-cooker meal.

*Serves 6*

### Large Bag

> ½ cup dehydrated cranberries
> 1 cup dehydrated cubed butternut squash
> ¼ cup dehydrated sliced onion
> 1 cup uncooked wild rice

### Small Bag

> 1 tablespoon chicken bouillon
> 1 teaspoon thyme

### To Store

Place all ingredients into bags. Place small bag into large bag, seal, and label with cooking instructions.

### Cooking Ingredients

> 1 pound turkey breast, cubed
> 8 cups warm water

### Directions

1. Sauté turkey in skillet until lightly browned, then place into slow cooker.
2. Pour ingredients from large bag only over the turkey.
3. Place ingredients from small bag into blender with the warm water and blend until dissolved.
4. Pour blended mixture into slow cooker.
5. Cook on high heat for 4 to 5 hours or low for 7 to 8 hours.

# Slow Southwest Casserole

A quick and easy Mexican slow-cooker meal.

*Serves 6*

*Large Bag*

> 2 cups uncooked white rice
> 1 cup dry kidney beans

*Small Bag*

> ½ cup dehydrated shredded onion
> 1 cup dehydrated sliced tomatoes
> ¼ cup dehydrated sliced black olives
> 2 tablespoons Taco Seasoning (see page 16)

*To Store*

Place all ingredients into bags. Place small bag into large bag, seal, and label with cooking instructions.

*Cooking Ingredients*

> 8 cups water
> 1 pound ground turkey, cooked

*Directions*

1. Place ingredients from large and small bags into slow cooker.
2. Add water and cooked ground turkey.
3. Cook on high heat 4 to 5 hours or low 7 to 8 hours

# Pineapple Pork and Rice

Sweet and savory rice dish that is an easy crowd-pleaser.

*Serves 10*

### Large Bag

> 6 cups uncooked long-grain rice
> 2 tablespoons BBQ Seasoning (see page 18)

### Small Bag

> 1 cup dehydrated pineapple tidbits
> 2 tablespoons dehydrated green bell peppers, chopped
> 2 tablespoons dehydrated red bell peppers, chopped

### To Store

Place all ingredients into bags. Place small bag into large bag, seal, and label with cooking instructions.

### Cooking Ingredients

> 10½ cups water
> 2 pounds pork loin, cubed
> 2 tablespoons honey

### Directions

1. Place large and small bags of dry ingredients into the slow cooker.
2. Add water and stir.
3. Add pork loin.
4. Cook on high heat 5 to 6 hours or low for 7 to 8 hours
5. Drizzle lightly with honey just before serving.

# Lentil Chicken Chili

It's easy to eat healthy with dehydrating. Case in point—this recipe.

*Serves 8*

*Large Bag*

> 1 cup dehydrated sliced onion
> 1 cup dehydrated cherry tomatoes, halved
> ½ cup dehydrated sliced carrots
> 1 tablespoon dehydrated sliced celery

*Small Bag*

> 1 cup dry lentils
> 2 tablespoons powdered dehydrated pumpkin
> 1 tablespoon chili powder
> 1 teaspoon ground cumin
> 1 teaspoon dried oregano
> ½ teaspoon dehydrated hot cherry pepper, crushed
> 2 teaspoons chicken bouillon

*To Store*

Place all ingredients into bags. Place small bag into large bag, seal, and label with cooking instructions.

*Cooking Ingredients*

> 10 cups water
> 2 cooked chicken breasts, cubed

*Directions*

1. Place all ingredients from large bag and small bag into the slow cooker.
2. Add water and chicken.
3. Cover and cook on high heat 5 to 6 hours or low for 8 to 9 hours.

# Black-Eyed Peas with Ham

A smoky and hearty main dish.

*Serves 10*

### Large Bag

> 2 cups black-eyed peas
>
> 4 cups uncooked long-grain rice
>
> 1 tablespoon powdered dehydrated tomato paste
>
> 2 teaspoons chicken bouillon
>
> 1½ teaspoons ground cumin

### Medium Bag

> ½ cup dehydrated thinly sliced carrots
>
> 2 tablespoons dehydrated chopped onion
>
> ½ cup dehydrated diced tomatoes
>
> 1 tablespoon dehydrated chopped green chiles
>
> 1 cup dehydrated chopped mustard greens

### To Store

Place all ingredients into bags. Place medium bag into large bag, seal, and label with cooking instructions.

### Cooking Ingredients

> 12 cups water
>
> 1 pound smoked ham, off the bone, cubed

### Directions

1. Place all ingredients from large and medium bags into a slow cooker with water, stir.
2. Add ham.
3. Cook on high heat 7 to 8 hours.

# Fiesta Chicken and Rice Bowls

Ditch the tortillas shells for these easy slow-cooker rice bowls.

*Serves 4*

## Large Bag

   2 cups uncooked rice
   2 cups dry black beans
   ½ cup dehydrated corn

## Small Bag

   ½ cup dehydrated diced tomatoes
   1 teaspoon dehydrated green chiles
   1 package Taco Seasoning (see page 16)
   1 teaspoon chicken bouillon

## To Store

Place all ingredients into bags. Place small bag into large bag, seal, and label with cooking instructions.

## Cooking Ingredients

   1½ pounds chicken breast, cubed
   9 cups water
   ¼ cup shredded Mexican-style cheese
   Sour cream (optional)

## Directions

1. Combine ingredients from large and small bags in slow cooker.
2. Add water, stir.
3. Add chicken.
4. Cook on high heat 5 to 6 hours.
5. Serve topped with shredded cheese and sour cream.

## Fun Tip

Do you have leftovers? Another great idea is to spoon ingredients into floured tortilla shells and serve as chicken burritos. Two meals in one!

# Citrus Dill Veggies and Rice

Just add water for this fast and easy 20-minute rice cooker meal.

*Serves 4*

### Large Bag

> 2 cups uncooked white rice
> ½ cup dehydrated shredded carrots
> ½ cup dehydrated shredded zucchini
> ½ cup dehydrated shredded summer squash
> ½ cup dehydrated sliced mushrooms

### Small Bag

> 2 tablespoons Citrus & Dill Seasoning (see page 16)

### To Store

Place all ingredients into bags. Place small bag into large bag, seal, and label with cooking instructions.

### Cooking Ingredients

> 8 cups water

### Directions

1. Place ingredients from large and small bags into rice cooker.
2. Add water, stir, and cover.
3. Cook 20 to 25 minutes until rice is tender and veggies hydrate.

# Tropical Fruit and Veggie Side Dish

Try this creative new side dish. Why do ordinary?

*Serves 4*

*Large Bag*

½ cup dehydrated sliced carrots

2½ cups dehydrated sliced apples

½ cup dehydrated pineapple tidbits

1 cup raisins

*Small Bag*

½ cup brown sugar

½ cup chopped pecans

¼ teaspoon ground cloves

1 teaspoon cinnamon

2 teaspoons cornstarch

*To Store*

Place all ingredients into bags. Place small bag into large bag, seal, and label with cooking instructions.

*Cooking Ingredients*

8½ cups water

1 tablespoon butter

*Directions*

1. Place ingredients from large and small bags into slow cooker.
2. Add water while stirring until well blended and powder is dissolved. Then add butter.
3. Cook on high heat for 4 to 5 hours or low for 7 to 8 hours.

# Southwest Rice and Veggies

Serve as the main course or as a side dish.

*Serves 8*

*Large Bag*

    1 cup uncooked white rice
    ½ cup dry black beans
    1 tablespoon Taco Seasoning (see page 16)

*Small Bag*

    1½ cups dehydrated halved cherry tomatoes
    ¼ cup dehydrated chopped chile peppers
    1 cup dehydrated corn
    ¼ cup dehydrated sliced black olives
    ½ cup dehydrated shredded onion

*To Store*

Place all ingredients into bags. Place small bag into large bag, seal, and label with cooking instructions.

*Cooking Ingredients*

    8 cups water
    Sour cream (optional)

*Directions*

1. Place ingredients from large and small bags into slow cooker, and add water.
2. Cook on high heat for 5 to 6 hours or low for 7 to 8 hours.
3. Serve with a dollop of sour cream if desired.

# Spicy Acorn Squash

Just add water for a spicy and sweet side dish!

*Serves 6*

### Large Bag

    3 cups dehydrated cubed acorn squash
    ½ cup raisins
    ¾ cup brown sugar
    1 teaspoon nutmeg
    1 teaspoon cinnamon
    ½ teaspoon crushed dehydrated hot red pepper

### To Store

Place all ingredients into large bag, seal, and label with cooking instructions.

### Cooking Ingredients

    7 cups water

### Directions

1. Pour ingredients from large bag into slow cooker, and add water.
2. Stir together and cover.
3. Cook on high heat for 4 to 5 hours or low for 7 to 8 hours.

# Basil Pesto Rice

Just add water for a delicious side dish, or add chicken for a complete main course.

*Serves 8*

### *Large Bag*

- 2 cups uncooked rice
- 2 tablespoons Basil Pesto Seasoning (see page 18) If adding the optional chicken, add an extra 2 teaspoons seasoning.

### *To Store*

Place all ingredients into large bag, seal, and label with cooking instructions.

### *Cooking Ingredients*

- 3¼ cups water
- 3 chicken breasts, cooked, cubed (optional)

### *Directions*

1. Pour ingredients from bag into a rice cooker and add water.
2. Stir, cover, then cook until rice is desired consistency.

# Apple and Sweet Potato Bake

This side dish is rich with sweet apples and potatoes.

*Serves 8*

*Large Bag*

> 4 cups dehydrated sliced apples
>
> 2 cups dehydrated sliced sweet potatoes

*Small Bag*

> 1 cup all-purpose flour
>
> 1 cup brown sugar
>
> 1 tablespoon Pumpkin Pie Spice (see page 23)

*To Store*

Place all ingredients into bags. Place small bag into large bag, seal, and label with cooking instructions.

*Cooking Ingredients*

> 8 cups boiling water
>
> ¼ cup (½ stick) butter

*Directions*

1. Place ingredients from large bag only into slow cooker.
2. Add boiling water to the slow cooker and let set 10 minutes.
3. Place ingredients from small bag into mixing bowl, then add butter and cut in the flour and brown sugar mixture until crumbly.
4. Sprinkle the crumble over the items in the slow cooker. Do not drain extra water.
5. Cover and cook on high heat for 4 to 5 hours or low for 7 to 8 hours.

# Broccoli-Mushroom-Cheese Rice

Just add water and eggs. Great as a side dish or a main dish.

*Serves 8*

*Large Bag*

> 2 cups rice

*Medium Bag*

> ¼ cup dehydrated broccoli florets
> ¼ cup dehydrated sliced mushrooms
> 2 tablespoons dehydrated chopped bell pepper
> 2 tablespoons dehydrated chopped onion

*Small Bag*

> 2 tablespoons powdered nonfat milk
> 1 cup powdered cheese

*To Store*

Place all ingredients into bags. Place smaller bags into large bag, seal, and label with cooking instructions.

*Cooking Ingredients*

> 7 cups warm water
> 3 eggs

*Directions*

1. Place ingredients from small bag into a blender with eggs and warm water, and blend until smooth.
2. Place ingredients from large and medium bags into slow cooker.
3. Pour ingredients from blender over top of rice and veggies. Stir, cover, and cook on high heat for 4 hours.

# Spanish Rice

Just add water to this homemade rice in a bag.

*Serves 6*

*Large Bag*

> ¼ cup dehydrated chopped onions
> ¼ cup dehydrated chopped red bell pepper
> ¼ cup dehydrated chopped green chiles
> 1 cup dehydrated chopped tomatoes
> 2 cups uncooked white rice
> 2 tablespoons Taco Seasoning (see page 16)

*To Store*

Place all ingredients into large bag, seal, and label with cooking instructions.

*Cooking Ingredients*

> 5½ cups water

*Directions*

1. Place ingredients from large bag into a rice cooker.
2. Add water, stir, cover, and cook 20 to 25 minutes until rice is fluffy and veggies are tender.

# Apple Crisp

This easy treat not only tastes great, it will enchant your house with the pleasant scents of autumn.

*Serves 6*

*Large Bag*

> 6 cups dehydrated sliced apples

*Small Bag*

> ¾ cup all-purpose flour
> 1 cup brown sugar
> ¾ cup rolled oats

*To Store*

Place all ingredients into bags. Place small bag into large bag, seal, and label with cooking instructions.

*Cooking Ingredients*

> 10 cups boiling water
> ¼ cup (½ stick) softened butter

*Directions*

1. Place ingredients from large bag only into slow cooker.
2. In slow cooker, stir in the boiling water, then cover and let set for 15 minutes.
3. Pour ingredients from small bag into a mixing bowl with butter.
4. Cut into mixture until it makes a crumble.
5. Sprinkle the crumble on top of apples in slow cooker.
6. Cook, covered, on high heat for 4 to 5 hours or low for 7 to 8 hours.

# Peach Bread Pudding

Try this recipe with different kinds of bread: French bread, donuts, cinnamon buns, or whatever is about to go stale. Cube and dehydrate these breads and use in place of plain breadcrumbs. You may discover something extraordinary!

*Serves 8*

## Large Bag

   8 cups dehydrated bread cubes

## Small Bag

   ½ cup golden white raisins
   2½ cups dehydrated sliced peaches, cut in half
   ¾ cup sugar

## To Store

Place all ingredients into bags. Place small bag into large bag, seal, and label with cooking instructions.

## Cooking Ingredients

   6 eggs
   8 cups milk (2 percent or whole)

## Directions

1. Grease slow cooker.
2. Pour ingredients from large and small bags into slow cooker.
3. Crack eggs and place into blender along with milk, then blend until smooth.
4. Pour blended mixture over ingredients in slow cooker, stir by hand for 1 minute, then cover.
5. Cook on low heat for 5 hours.

# Hawaiian Bread Pudding

Try this recipe with different kinds of bread: French bread, donuts, cinnamon buns, or whatever is about to go stale. Cube and dehydrate these breads and use in place of plain breadcrumbs. This is a delicious tropical treat.

*Serves 8*

*Large Bag*

    8 cups dehydrated bread cubes

*Small Bag*

    ½ cup dehydrated flaked coconut
    1 cup dehydrated pineapple tidbits
    1 cup dehydrated sliced banana

*To Store*

Place all ingredients into bags. Place small bag into large bag, seal, and label with cooking instructions.

*Cooking Ingredients*

    6 eggs
    8 cups milk (2 percent or whole)

*Directions*

1. Grease slow cooker.
2. Pour ingredients from large and small bags into slow cooker.
3. Crack eggs and place into blender along with milk, then blend until smooth.
4. Pour blended mixture over ingredients in slow cooker, stir by hand for 1 minute, then cover.
5. Cook on low heat for 5 hours.

# Peach and Raisin Rice Pudding

Just add water and watch this creamy rice pudding come to life.

*Serves 8*

### Large Bag

  1 cup dehydrated sliced peaches
  1 cup raisins

### Small Bag

  2 cups uncooked white rice
  ¾ cup white sugar
  ¼ cup brown sugar
  1½ cups powdered nonfat milk

### To Store

Place all ingredients into bags. Place small bag into large bag, seal, and label with cooking instructions.

### Cooking Ingredients

  8 cups warm water

### Directions

1. Grease slow cooker.
2. Pour ingredients from large and small bags into slow cooker.
3. Add warm water, stir for 1 minute, then cover.
4. Cook on high heat for 3½ to 4 hours.

# Apple-Raisin and Banana Bread Pudding

Try this recipe with different kinds of bread: French bread, donuts, cinnamon buns, or whatever is about to go stale. Cube and dehydrate these breads and use in place of plain breadcrumbs. Include a little something unexpected by adding banana to an apple-raisin treat.

*Serves 6*

### Large Bag

8 cups dehydrated ½-inch cubed white bread

### Small Bag

½ cup raisins
½ cup dehydrated sliced apples, cut in half
1 cup dehydrated sliced bananas
¾ cup sugar
1 teaspoon cinnamon

### To Store

Place all ingredients into bags. Place small bag into large bag, seal, and label with cooking instructions.

### Cooking Ingredients

6 eggs
8 cups milk

### Directions

1. Grease slow cooker.
2. Pour ingredients from large and small bags into slow cooker.
3. Crack eggs and place into blender along with milk, then blend until smooth.
4. Pour blended mixture over ingredients in slow cooker, stir by hand for 1 minute, then cover.
5. Cook on high heat for 4 hours.

# Apple-Peach Pudding Bread

Delicious. Moist. Light. Heavenly.

*Serves 8*

*Large Bag*

> 2 cups flour
> 1½ cups sugar
> 2 teaspoons baking soda
> 1 teaspoon baking powder
> ½ teaspoon salt
> ¼ cup powdered nonfat milk

*Small Bag*

> ½ cup dehydrated thinly sliced apples
> ½ cup dehydrated thinly sliced peaches

*To Store*

Place all ingredients into bags. Place small bag into large bag, seal, and label with cooking instructions.

*Cooking Ingredients*

> 2 cups boiling water
> 2 eggs
> ¾ cup oil
> ¾ cup water

*Directions*

1. Place ingredients from small bag into a bowl.
2. Add boiling water, cover, and let cool. Lightly drain any extra water (do not press or squeeze when draining).
3. Place ingredients from large bag into a separate mixing bowl.
4. Add eggs, oil, and ¾ cup water, and blend until smooth.
5. Fold in hydrated peaches and apples.
6. Pour batter into slow cooker that has been sprayed with cooking oil.
7. Cover and cook on high heat for 3 hours.
8. Leaving cover on, let cool for 30 minutes, then serve.

# Chapter 7

# Meals in a Bag

Similar to pour-and-go meals, these recipes are for premade bagged meals for your storage. The difference is instead of using a slow cooker or rice cooker so you can just pour and go, meals in a bag are for you to use at dinnertime to whip together a beautiful and robust meal in a snap! You will make your family and guests think that you have been slaving in the kitchen for hours making these flavorful dishes. We'll let that part be our little secret!

# "So Simple" Roasted Red Pepper and Gouda Soup

This creamy soup is full of flavor and will top your list of comfort foods.

*Serves 4*

### Small Bag

> 4 teaspoons chicken bouillon
> 2 tablespoon Spicy Roasted Red Pepper Seasoning (see page 17)

### To Store

Place all ingredients into small bag. Place up to 4 small bags into a large Mylar bag, seal, and label with cooking instructions.

### Cooking Ingredients

> 4 cups water
> ½ cup shredded Gouda cheese

### Directions

1. In a 4-quart saucepan, add water and contents of small bag. Bring to a boil.
2. Let simmer and reduce, uncovered, for 15 minutes.
3. Fold in gouda, stirring frequently until all cheese has melted.

# Crab Chowder

Easy chowder that can be made with or without the crab.

*Serves 6*

### Large Bag

½ cup dehydrated corn
½ cup dehydrated sliced onions
¼ cup dehydrated chopped green bell pepper
⅛ cup dehydrated diced carrots
1 cup dehydrated small cubed red potatoes with peelings

### Small Bag

1 cup powdered milk
1 tablespoon dehydrated parsley, crushed
1½ teaspoons seafood seasoning
½ teaspoon dried thyme
1 teaspoon flour

### To Store

Place all ingredients into bags. Place small bag into large bag, seal, and label with cooking instructions.

### Cooking Ingredients

8½ cups water
1 cup crab meat (use real or imitation crab)

### Directions

1. Add ingredients from large and small bags into medium pot.
2. Add water and stir.
3. Bring to boil, cover, reduce heat, and simmer 40 minutes.
4. Add crab, cover, and cook an additional 10 minutes.

# Carrot, Corn, and Cherry Tomato Soup

Just add water to create this flavorful veggie tomato soup.

*Serves 4*

*Large Bag*

    ¼ cup dehydrated sliced carrots
    ¼ cup dehydrated thinly sliced fennel
    ½ cup dehydrated halved cherry tomatoes
    ¼ cup dehydrated corn
    2 teaspoons dehydrated crushed oregano
    1 tablespoon chicken bouillon

*Small Bag*

    1 cup rice

*To Store*

Place all ingredients into bags. Place small bag into large bag, seal, and label with cooking instructions.

*Cooking Ingredients*

    8 cups water

*Directions*

1.  Place ingredients from large and small bags into a pot.
2.  Add water, bring to a boil, cover, and reduce heat to simmer 45 minutes.

# Spanish Chicken & Olive Soup

This Spanish-style soup is a great change of pace from ordinary chicken soup.

*Serves 6*

### Large Bag

> 2 tablespoons dehydrated sliced green olives
> ¼ cup dehydrated chopped tomato
> ½ cup dehydrated chopped onion
> ½ teaspoon dehydrated chopped garlic
> ¼ teaspoon dehydrated crushed red pepper
> 1 tablespoon dehydrated chopped basil
> 1 cup uncooked white rice

### To Store

Place all ingredients into large bag, seal, and label with cooking instructions.

### Cooking Ingredients

> 6½ cups water
> 1 cooked chicken breast, shredded

### Directions

1. Add all ingredients into a pot with water and chicken.
2. Bring to a boil, cover, reduce to simmer, and cook 30 minutes or until vegetables and rice are tender.

# Corn & Red Potato Soup

Just add water for this savory soup with a subtle sweetness.

*Serves 6*

*Large Bag*

> 1 cup dehydrated diced red potatoes with peel
> ½ cup dehydrated shredded onion
> 1 tablespoon dehydrated thinly sliced celery
> ½ cup dehydrated corn

*Small Bag*

> 1½ cups powdered milk
> 1 teaspoon cornstarch

*To Store*

Place all ingredients into bags. Place small bag into large bag, seal, and label with cooking instructions.

*Cooking Ingredients*

> 8½ cups water

*Directions*

1. Place all ingredients from large and small bags into pot. Add water.
2. Bring to boil, cover, reduce heat to simmer, and cook 1 hour until potatoes and corn are tender.

# Southwest Corn and Turkey Soup

This zesty soup pairs well with the subtle sweetness of corn.

*Serves 6*

### Large Bag

> 1 cup dehydrated sliced zucchini, cut in half
> ¼ cup dehydrated sliced onions
> ¼ cup dehydrated corn
> ¼ cup dry black beans
> ¼ cup dehydrated chiles

### Small Bag

> ½ teaspoon garlic powder
> 1 teaspoon ground cumin
> ¼ cup cornmeal
> 1 teaspoon dehydrated oregano
> 1 teaspoon dehydrated parsley, crushed

### To Store

Place all ingredients into bags. Place small bag into large bag, seal, and label with cooking instructions.

### Cooking Ingredients

> 2 cups cooked shredded turkey

### Directions

1. Place ingredients from large and small bags into a medium pot with water. Cover. Bring to a boil, reduce heat. Simmer 30 minutes, stirring occasionally.
2. Add shredded turkey. Cover and simmer for an additional 10 minutes.

# Spicy Chicken and Squash Soup

Just add water and chicken to this soup in a bag.

*Serves 4*

### Large Bag

> 1 cup dehydrated cubed butternut squash
> ¼ cup dehydrated diced tomatoes
> 1 tablespoon dehydrated chopped onions
> ½ teaspoon dehydrated diced chiles
> ½ teaspoon dehydrated lemon zest

### Small Bag

> ½ teaspoon ground ginger
> ⅛ teaspoon black pepper
> ½ teaspoon dehydrated parsley, crushed
> ⅛ teaspoon cumin
> ¼ teaspoon salt

### To Store

Place all ingredients into bags. Place small bag into large bag, seal, and label with cooking instructions.

### Cooking Ingredients

> 6 cups water
> 2 cooked chicken breasts, cubed

### Directions

1. Place ingredients from large and small bags into medium pot.
2. Add water and cubed chicken.
3. Bring to a boil, cover, and simmer 40 minutes.

# Curried Chicken and Vegetable Soup

Brimming with flavor and loaded with vegetables.

*Serves 6*

*Large Bag*

>  2 cups egg noodles

*Small Bag*

>  2 tablespoons dehydrated diced carrots
>  2 tablespoons dehydrated diced onions
>  2 tablespoons dehydrated peas
>  2 tablespoons dehydrated broccoli florets
>  ½ teaspoon dry mustard
>  ½ teaspoon chili powder
>  ¼ teaspoon curry powder
>  2 teaspoons chicken bouillon

*To Store*

Place all ingredients into bags. Place small bag into large bag, seal, and label with cooking instructions.

*Cooking Ingredients*

>  6 cups water
>  2 cooked chicken breasts, shredded

*Directions*

1.  Place ingredients from small bag into a pot with water and cover. Bring to boil and reduce heat to simmer for 20 minutes.
2.  Increase heat to medium. Add chicken.
3.  Add ingredients from large bag to pot, cover, and cook an additional 10 minutes.

# Cheesy Broccoli Soup

Just add water for this classic and creamy family favorite.

*Serves 6*

*Large Bag*

   ½ cup powdered dehydrated broccoli
   ½ cup dehydrated broccoli florets
   2 tablespoons dehydrated chopped onion

*Small Bag*

   1 cup powdered white cheddar cheese
   ¾ cup powdered nonfat milk

*To Store*

Place all ingredients into bags. Place small bag into large bag, seal, and label with cooking instructions.

*Cooking Ingredients*

   8 cups water

*Directions*

1. Place ingredients from large and small bags into pot. Add water.
2. Bring to a boil, cover, reduce heat to simmer, and cook 30 minutes.

# Spinach & Tomato Penne Soup

A flavorful and versatile soup. Serve with a crisped baguette.

*Serves 6*

*Large Bag*

> 2 cups small penne pasta

*Medium Bag*

> 2 cups dehydrated baby spinach
> 1 cup dehydrated halved cherry tomatoes

*Small Bag*

> 1 tablespoon powdered dehydrated tomato paste
> 2 tablespoon Spicy Roasted Red Pepper Seasoning (see page 17)

*To Store*

Place all ingredients into bags. Place small bag into large bag, seal, and label with cooking instructions.

*Cooking Ingredients*

> 8 cups water

*Directions*

1. Place ingredients from both medium and small bags into pot with water. Bring to a boil.
2. Add ingredients from large bag, reduce heat to medium, and cook until penne pasta is tender, 10 to 15 minutes.

# Cheeseburger Soup

An American classic, now in a fast, rich, and creamy soup.

*Serves 6*

*Large Bag*

¼ cup dehydrated sliced tomatoes
¼ cup dehydrated sliced sweet pickles
¼ cup dehydrated sliced onions
1 cup dehydrated shredded potatoes (hash browns)

*Medium Bag*

1 cup powdered cheese
½ cup powdered milk
½ teaspoon dry mustard
2 teaspoons powdered dehydrated tomato paste

*To Store*

Place all ingredients into bags. Place medium bag into large bag, seal, and label with cooking instructions.

*Cooking Ingredients*

1 pound ground beef
6 cups water

*Directions*

1. Cook ground beef in a skillet, drain, and set aside.
2. Place ingredients from large and medium bags into a pot. Add water, stir, bring to boil, and reduce heat to simmer.
3. Add cooked ground beef, cover, and cook 20 to 25 minutes.

# Taco Soup

Easy Mexican-style soup.

*Serves 6*

### Large Bag

> 2 cups dehydrated refried beans
> ¼ cup dehydrated chopped tomatoes
> 1 tablespoon dehydrated chopped onions
> 1 teaspoon dehydrated chopped green chiles
> 1 tablespoon Taco Seasoning (see page 16)
> 1 teaspoon dehydrated crushed garlic
> ½ teaspoon salt
> ½ teaspoon black pepper

### Small Bag

> 4 crushed taco shells

### To Store

Place all ingredients into bags. Place small bag into large bag, seal, and label with cooking instructions.

### Cooking Ingredients

> 6 cups water
> 1 pound cooked ground beef, drained

### Directions

1. Place ingredients from large bag into medium pot. Add water. Bring to a boil, cover, reduce heat, and simmer 30 minutes.
2. Add ground beef. Cover and cook an additional 10 minutes.
3. Place each serving into small bowl and top with crumbled taco shells from small bag.

# Lasagna Soup

Two comfort foods, lasagna and hot soup, rolled into one. Dream no further.

*Serves 6*

### *Large Bag*

> **16 pieces small no-boil lasagna noodles (see page 11)**

### *Medium Bag*

> **16 dehydrated zucchini slices**
> **16 dehydrated tomato slices**
> **¼ cup dehydrated sliced onion**
> **½ teaspoon crushed red peppers**
> **1 tablespoon dehydrated basil**
> **2 teaspoons Italian Seasoning (see page 19)**
> **1 tablespoon powdered dehydrated tomato paste**
> **2 teaspoons chicken bouillon**
> **½ teaspoon dehydrated crushed garlic**

### *To Store*

Place all ingredients into bags. Place medium bag into large bag, seal, and label with cooking instructions.

### *Cooking Ingredients*

> **8 cups water**
> **1 pound cooked ground beef, drained**
> **Parmesan cheese (optional)**

### *Directions*

1. Place ingredients from both medium and large bags into large pot. Add water and ground beef.
2. Cover, bring to boil, reduce heat to simmer, and cook 30 to 35 minutes.
3. Serve with Parmesan cheese sprinkled on top if desired.

# Hearty Chicken & Veggie Soup

Loaded with chicken and vegetables. Packed with flavor.

*Serves 8*

### Large Bag

- ¼ cup dehydrated peas
- ¼ cup dehydrated thinly sliced carrots
- ¼ cup dehydrated cut green beans
- ½ cup dehydrated sliced and halved summer squash
- ¼ cup dehydrated halved cherry tomatoes
- ¼ cup dehydrated corn

### Small Bag

- 2 cubes chicken bouillon
- ⅛ teaspoon dried thyme
- ⅛ teaspoon dried rosemary
- ⅛ teaspoon black pepper
- 1 teaspoon dehydrated parsley, crushed

### To Store

Place all ingredients into bags. Place small bag into large bag, seal, and label with cooking instructions.

### Cooking Ingredients

- 2 cooked chicken breasts, shredded

### Directions

1. Add the ingredients from large and small bags to medium pot. Add water, bring to a boil, cover, reduce heat, and simmer 40 minutes. Stir occasionally.
2. Add cooked shredded chicken, cover, and simmer for 10 additional minutes.

# Island Vegetable and Rice Soup

A light and tropical soup. Just add water . . . and an ocean breeze.

*Serves 6*

*Large Bag*

- ¼ cup dehydrated broccoli florets
- ¼ cup dehydrated snow peas
- ¼ cup dehydrated sliced sweet red pepper
- ¼ cup dehydrated thinly sliced carrots
- 1 cup uncooked instant brown rice

*Small Bag*

- 2 teaspoons curry powder
- ½ teaspoon crushed dehydrated red cherry pepper
- ½ teaspoons salt
- 1 teaspoon dehydrated lime zest
- 1 tablespoon dehydrated shredded coconut

*To Store*

Place all ingredients into bags. Place small bag into large bag, seal, and label with cooking instructions.

*Cooking Ingredients*

- 8 cups water

*Directions*

1. Add ingredients from large and small bags to a medium pot. Add water.
2. Bring to a boil, reduce heat to a simmer, cover, and cook 40 minutes, stirring occasionally.

# Minestrone Soup

Your daily dose of vegetables in a hearty classic Italian favorite.

*Serves 8*

### Large Bag

 2 cups dehydrated baby leaf spinach
 ½ cup dehydrated sliced, halved zucchini
 ¼ cup dehydrated sliced onion
 ½ cup dehydrated chickpeas
 ¼ cup dehydrated thinly sliced carrots
 ⅓ cup dehydrated sliced tomatoes

### Small Bag

 1 cup uncooked macaroni noodles
 1 tablespoon powdered dehydrated tomato paste
 1 teaspoon dehydrated crushed basil
 ¾ teaspoon black pepper
 ¾ teaspoon salt
 1 teaspoon crushed dehydrated oregano
 1 tablespoon dehydrated chopped celery

### To Store

Place all ingredients into bags. Place small bag into large bag, seal, and label with cooking instructions.

### Cooking Ingredients

 10 cups water

### Directions

1. Place ingredients from large and small bags into medium pot. Add water.
2. Bring to a boil, reduce heat to a simmer, cover, and cook 40 minutes, stirring occasionally.

# Quinoa-Veggie Soup

Just add water and this flavorsome soup is ready in less than 30 minutes.

*Serves 6*

*Large Bag*

  2 tablespoons dehydrated corn
  2 tablespoons dehydrated shredded carrots
  1 cup dehydrated kale
  ½ cup dehydrated sliced tomatoes
  ½ teaspoon dehydrated diced hot cherry pepper
  1 tablespoon dehydrated diced onion
  1 teaspoon dehydrated basil
  2 teaspoons vegetable bouillon
  ½ tablespoon curry powder
  1 cup quinoa

*To Store*

Place all ingredients into large bag, seal, and label with cooking instructions.

*Cooking Ingredients*

  7 cups water

*Directions*

1. Place ingredients from large bag into a pot.
2. Add water, bring to a boil, cover, and reduce heat to simmer for 20 minutes.

# Portobello Soup

A full-bodied soup, ready in less than 30 minutes.

*Serves 4*

*Large Bag*

>  1 cup dehydrated sliced tomatoes
>  2 cups dehydrated sliced portobello mushrooms
>  ¼ cup dehydrated shredded onion
>  2 cups dehydrated kale
>  ½ teaspoon dried rosemary
>  ½ teaspoon dried basil
>  1 bay leaf
>  1 teaspoon dried thyme
>  ¼ teaspoon pepper
>  1 tablespoon vegetable bouillon

*To Store*

Place all ingredients into large bag, seal, and label with cooking instructions.

*Cooking Ingredients*

>  6½ cups water

*Directions*

1. Place ingredients from large bag into a pot.
2. Add water, bring to a boil, cover, and reduce heat to simmer for 20 minutes.

# Spinach Soup

A mellow and healthy soup, ready in less than 30 minutes.

*Serves 4*

*Large Bag*

   3 cups dehydrated spinach
   3 cups dehydrated arugula
   1 cup dehydrated parsley
   1 cup dehydrated shredded onion
   3 teaspoons chicken bouillon

*To Store*

Place all ingredients into large bag, seal, and label with cooking instructions.

*Cooking Ingredients*

   7 cups water

*Directions*

1. Place ingredients from large bag into a pot.
2. Add water, bring to a boil, cover, and reduce heat to simmer for 20 minutes.

# Chicken & Spinach Pasta

Just add water and chicken to this creamy pasta.

*Serves 4*

*Large Bag*

   2 cups uncooked spiral pasta (see page 12)

*Medium Bag*

   ¼ cup dehydrated sliced mushrooms
   ½ cup dehydrated halved cherry tomatoes
   1 cup dehydrated spinach

*Small Bag*

   2 teaspoons chicken bouillon powder
   ½ teaspoon dehydrated oregano
   ¼ cup powdered cheese
   ½ cup powdered milk

*To Store*

Place all ingredients into bags. Place smaller bags into large bag, seal, and label with cooking instructions.

*Cooking Ingredients*

   5 cups water
   2 cooked chicken breasts, cubed

*Directions*

1. Add all ingredients from large, medium, and small bags into a large skillet.
2. Add water and cubed chicken.
3. Stir all ingredients together in skillet. Bring to a boil, cover, and simmer 15 to 20 minutes.

# Shepherd's Pie

This easy classic Irish dish puts the "comfort" in comfort food.

*Serves 6*

*Large Bag*

   3 cups instant potatoes

*Medium Bag*

   ¼ cup dehydrated corn
   ¼ cup dehydrated peas
   ¼ cup dehydrated chopped carrots
   ¼ cup dehydrated shredded onions
   ¼ cup dehydrated chopped green bell pepper
   ¼ cup dehydrated sliced tomatoes

*Small Bag*

   4 teaspoons beef bouillon
   2 tablespoons cornstarch
   ¼ teaspoon ground pepper

*To Store*

Place all ingredients into bags. Place smaller bags into large bag, seal, and label with cooking instructions.

*Cooking Ingredients*

   1 cup boiling water
   1 tablespoon butter
   1 pound ground beef
   7 cups water
   3 eggs

*Directions*

1. Place large bag of instant potatoes into a bowl. Add 1 cup boiling water and butter. Gently fold with fork. Set aside to cool.
2. Place ground beef in a Dutch oven over medium-high heat and scramble until brown. Drain grease.
3. Add ingredients from both medium and small bags into Dutch oven with cooked ground beef. Add 7 cups water, stir until blended, cover, bring to a boil, and reduce heat to simmer for 40 minutes.
4. Preheat oven to 400°F.
5. Add eggs to instant potatoes, mix together until smooth, and pour over top of beef and veggie mixture in Dutch oven.
6. Place into preheated oven (do not cover). Bake for 25 minutes or until top is a crispy golden brown.

# Apricot Chicken

A fast and delicious entrée, ready in 20 minutes!

*Serves 4*

### Large Bag

> 2 cups dehydrated chopped apricots
> ½ cup dehydrated shredded carrots
> 1 teaspoon dehydrated crushed garlic
> 1 teaspoon cinnamon

### To Store

Place all ingredients into large bag, seal, and label with cooking instructions.

### Cooking Ingredients

> 4 cups water
> 2 tablespoons butter
> ½ tablespoon olive oil
> 4 chicken breasts

### Directions

1. Place ingredients from large bag into a pot. Add water and butter, bring to a boil, and reduce heat to simmer for 20 minutes.
2. In a skillet, heat olive oil over medium heat, place chicken breasts in skillet, and brown each side 4 to 5 minutes until golden brown and thoroughly cooked.
3. Spoon apricot mixture over each chicken breast and serve.

# Chicken and Stuffing Casserole

Quick and easy one-dish meal.

*Serves 8*

*Large Bag*

> 10 cups dehydrated ½-inch bread cubes

*Medium Bag*

> 2 cups dehydrated shredded potatoes
> 1 cup dehydrated parsley
> 1 cup dehydrated sliced mushrooms
> ½ cup dehydrated chopped red bell pepper

*Small Bag*

> 2 tablespoons chicken bouillon
> 1 cup powdered nonfat milk
> ½ cup powdered cheese

*To Store*

Place all ingredients into bags. Place smaller bags into large bag, seal, and label with cooking instructions.

*Cooking Ingredients*

> 5 eggs
> 9 cups water
> 3 tablespoons butter
> 4 chicken breasts, cubed

*Directions*

1. Preheat oven to 350°F. Place contents of small bag into a blender. Add eggs, water, and butter. Blend until smooth.
2. Place contents of medium and large bags into a well-greased, deep 9 x 13-inch casserole dish.
3. Add chicken.
4. Pour mixture from blender over top of ingredients in casserole dish, and lightly stir.
5. Place into preheated oven and bake for 55 minutes until golden brown.

# Crab Cake Bake

All the flavors of a wonderful crab cake in a meal.

*Serves 8*

*Large Bag*

> 1 cup dehydrated ½-inch white bread cubes

*Small Bag*

> ½ cup dehydrated chopped red bell pepper
> ¼ cup dehydrated chopped onion
> 2 tablespoons dehydrated crushed parsley
> 1 teaspoon Old Bay seasoning

*To Store*

Place all ingredients into bags. Place small bag into large bag, seal, and label with cooking instructions.

*Cooking Ingredients*

> 8 ounces crabmeat or imitation crab
> 2 cups shredded cheddar cheese
> 8 eggs
> 2 cups half-and-half

*Directions*

1. Preheat oven to 350ºF. Place ingredients from large and small bags into a mixing bowl.
2. Add crabmeat and shredded cheddar cheese. Set aside.
3. In a blender, place eggs and half-and-half, and blend until smooth.
4. Pour mixture from blender over ingredients in mixing bowl, lightly mix.
5. Pour mixture into a 9 x 13-inch greased baking dish.
6. Place into preheated oven and bake for 35 minutes.

## Fun Tip

Try adding a dollop of flvored mayo from the spice chapter as a finishing touch such as Roasted Red Pepper Mayo, also known as an aioli.

## Fun Tip

Do you have leftovers? Use the leftover crab cake bake as a stuffing inside flounder. Two meals in one!

# Ranch Potato Ham Bake

This creamy ham and potato bake becomes addictive when you add ranch seasoning.

*Serves 6*

*Large Bag*

> 3 cups dehydrated sliced potatoes
> ½ cup dehydrated peas
> ¼ cup dehydrated shredded onions
> ¼ cup dehydrated mushrooms

*Small Bag*

> 2 teaspoons vegetable bouillon
> 1 tablespoon Ranch Seasoning (see page 22)
> 1 tablespoon cornstarch
> 3 tablespoons nonfat powdered milk

*To Store*

Place all ingredients into bags. Place small bag into large bag, seal, and label with cooking instructions.

*Cooking Ingredients*

> 8 cups boiling water
> 2 cups cubed ham

*Directions*

1. Preheat oven to 350°F. Place ingredients from large bag into a 3-quart greased Dutch oven.
2. Add boiling water and ingredients from small bag, and stir until dissolved.
3. Add ham.
4. Cover and place Dutch oven into preheated oven. Bake covered for 45 minutes. Remove the cover and place back in oven for an additional 15 minutes or until top is golden brown.

# Stovetop Tuna-Spinach-Noodle

Quick and easy tuna noodle casserole on the stove.

*Serves 4*

*Large Bag*

- 2 cups uncooked elbow macaroni
- ½ cup dehydrated sliced mushrooms

*Medium Bag*

- 1 cup dehydrated baby spinach
- 1 tablespoon dehydrated chopped onions
- 1 tablespoon dehydrated chopped pimientos

*Small Bag*

- 1 teaspoon ground mustard
- 6 tablespoons nonfat powdered milk
- ¼ cup powdered cheese

*To Store*

Place all ingredients into bags. Place smaller bags into large bag, seal, and label with cooking instructions.

*Cooking Ingredients*

- 8 cups water
- 2 tablespoons butter
- 1 (5-ounce) can tuna in water, drained

*Directions*

1. Bring a pot with 8 cups of water to a boil
2. Add ingredients from large bag; cook 10 minutes or until noodles are tender.
3. Drain water, reserving ⅔ cup pasta water for sauce.
4. Add butter and reserved pasta water and stir.
5. Add ingredients from small bag and stir.
6. Add ingredients from medium bag, stir, and continue to cook until thickened.
7. Fold in tuna. Serve hot.

# Italian Sausage and Pepper-Tomato Bake

Easy classic Italian dish.

*Serves 8*

*Large Bag*

>   2 cups dehydrated shredded onions
>   2 cups dehydrated shredded green bell peppers
>   2 cups dehydrated sliced tomatoes
>   ½ cup dehydrated sliced mushrooms

*Medium Bag*

>   16 pieces small no-boil lasagna noodles (see page 11)

*Small Bag*

>   1 tablespoon Italian Seasoning (see page 19)
>   3 tablespoons powdered dehydrated tomato paste

*To Store*

Place all ingredients into bags. Place smaller bags into large bag, seal, and label with cooking instructions.

*Cooking Ingredients*

>   10 cups water
>   2 pounds cooked Italian sausage, scrambled and drained
>   2 cups shredded mozzarella cheese

*Directions*

1. Preheat oven to 350°F. Place ingredients from medium and large bags into a 6-quart Dutch oven and add water.
2. Add ingredients from small bag into Dutch oven, and stir until dissolved.
3. Add sausage and stir.
4. Sprinkle cheese on top.
5. Cover, and bake in preheated oven for 55 minutes or until golden brown and bubbling.

# Spicy Stovetop Mac & Cheese

Kick up your mac and cheese with just a few simple ingredients.

*Serves 4*

### Large Bag

2 cups macaroni

### Small Bag

½ tablespoon Spicy Roasted Red Pepper Seasoning (see page 17)
⅓ cup powdered cheese
½ teaspoon cornstarch

### To Store

Place all ingredients into bags. Place small bag into large bag, seal, and label with cooking instructions.

### Cooking Ingredients

1 tablespoon butter
½ cup milk

### Directions

1. Bring a large pot of water to a boil and add ingredient from large bag. Cook 6 to 8 minutes, then drain.
2. Stir in butter and milk.
3. Add ingredients from small bag to pot.
4. Cook on low heat, stirring until creamy, approximately 1 to 2 minutes; serve.

# Sausage-Potato Bake

Easy casserole dish that the whole family will love!

*Serves 6*

*Large Bag*

   3 cups dehydrated sliced potatoes
   ½ cup dehydrated sliced plum tomatoes
   ¼ cup dehydrated sliced onions

*Small Bag*

   1½ teaspoons salt
   ¼ teaspoon black pepper
   1 tablespoon dehydrated chopped chives
   1 teaspoon dehydrated oregano
   1 tablespoon flour

*To Store*

Place all ingredients into bags. Place small bag into large bag, seal, and label with cooking instructions.

*Cooking Ingredients*

   ½ pound cooked pork sausage, crumbled and drained
   5 cups boiling water
   1 cup milk

*Directions*

1. Preheat oven to 350ºF.
2. Pour contents of large bag into an 8 x 10-inch greased baking dish. Add boiling water, cover, and let set 15 minutes.
3. Toss cooked sausage into casserole dish, lightly mixing with the veggies.
4. Place ingredients from small bag into blender with milk and blend until smooth.
5. Pour contents of blender over ingredients in baking dish and cover with foil. Place in preheated oven and bake for 40 minutes.
6. Remove foil and place back into oven for an additional 15 to 20 minutes or until golden brown.

# Veggie-Noodle Casserole

This dish is great as is, or try it with some shredded turkey for added protein.

*Serves 6*

### Large Bag

   2 cups uncooked macaroni
   ¼ cup dehydrated peas
   ¼ cup dehydrated corn
   2 tablespoons dehydrated chopped red bell peppers
   ¼ cup dehydrated shredded onions
   ¼ cup dehydrated sliced mushrooms

### Small Bag

   3 tablespoons nonfat powdered milk
   ½ cup powdered cheese
   1 teaspoon cornstarch
   1 tablespoon Sweet Caramelized Onion Seasoning (see page 21)

### To Store

Place all ingredients into bags. Place small bag into large bag, seal, and label with cooking instructions.

### Cooking Ingredients

   11 cups water, divided
   2 tablespoons butter
   1 cup Savory Sage and Onion Breadcrumbs (see page 25) (optional)

### Directions

1. Preheat oven to 350°F.
2. Place ingredients from small bag into blender. Add 3 cups water and butter, blend until smooth, and set aside.
3. Place ingredients from large bag into a pot. Add 8 cups water, bring to boil, cook 10 minutes, and drain water.
4. Pour batter from blender into the pot with cooked veggies; fold in until mixed. Pour into a 10 x 10-inch greased casserole dish.
5. Sprinkle top of dish with breadcrumbs (optional).
6. Place in a preheated oven for 35 minutes or until bubbly and golden brown.

# Chicken, Peas, and Carrots Casserole

A classic casserole that's an easy family pleaser.

*Serves 4*

*Large Bag*

    2 cups dehydrated ½-inch bread cubes

*Medium Bag*

    ¼ cup dehydrated chopped potatoes
    ¼ cup dehydrated peas
    ¼ cup dehydrated chopped carrots
    1 teaspoon dehydrated chopped celery

*Small Bag*

    ⅓ cup flour
    3 tablespoons powdered nonfat milk
    4 teaspoons chicken bouillon
    ½ teaspoon crushed dehydrated sage
    ½ teaspoon ground pepper

*To Store*

Place all ingredients into bags. Place smaller bags into large bag, seal, and label with cooking instructions.

*Cooking Ingredients*

    6 cups water
    2 cooked chicken breasts, cubed
    2 tablespoons butter, melted

*Directions*

1. Place ingredients from both medium and small bags into a pot. Add water, stir until smooth, bring to a boil, cover, and reduce heat to simmer for 20 minutes.
2. Add chicken.
3. Preheat oven to 350°F.
4. Grease a 10 x 10-inch casserole dish. Place ingredients from large bag into a mixing bowl with butter, and toss together until crumbs are coated with the butter.
5. Pour veggie and chicken mixture into greased casserole dish.
6. Sprinkle breadcrumbs over the top of chicken and veggies.
7. Place in preheated oven and bake 20 to 25 minutes or until bubbling and golden brown.

# Italian Bake

Italian pasta dish loaded with veggies.

*Serves 8*

### Large Bag

> 2 cups dehydrated sliced zucchini
> 2 cups dehydrated sliced summer squash
> 2 cups dehydrated sliced tomatoes
> 1 cup dehydrated shredded onion
> 2 tablespoons Italian Seasoning (see page 19)

### Small bag

> 16 pieces small no-boil lasagna noodles (see page 11)

### To Store

Place all ingredients into bags. Place small bag into large bag, seal, and label with cooking instructions.

### Cooking Ingredients

> 6 cups boiling water
> 1 pound cooked ground beef, scrambled and drained
> 1 (24-ounce) jar spaghetti sauce
> 2 cups shredded mozzarella

### Directions

1. Preheat oven to 350°F.
2. Place ingredients from large and small bags into a 6-quart greased baking dish.
3. Add boiling water, stir, and let set 10 minutes.
4. Add cooked ground beef and jar of spaghetti sauce. Stir gently.
5. Sprinkle with mozzarella cheese.
6. Placed dish into preheated oven for 55 minutes or until bubbling and golden brown.

# Hamburger-Noodle Skillet

An easy one-skillet meal in just 20 minutes that your kids will love.

*Serves 4*

*Large Bag*

>    2½ cups uncooked macaroni noodles

*Small Bag*

>    ½ cup dehydrated sliced mushrooms
>    ½ cup dehydrated sliced tomatoes
>    2 tablespoons dehydrated chopped onion
>    3 teaspoons beef bouillon
>    2 teaspoons cornstarch

*To Store*

Place all ingredients into bags. Place small bag into large bag, seal, and label with cooking instructions.

*Cooking Ingredients*

>    1 pound ground beef
>    6 cups water

*Directions*

1. Cook ground beef in a large skillet; drain.
2. Add water to ground beef.
3. Add ingredients from small bag to skillet and bring to a boil.
4. Add ingredients from large bag, cover, reduce heat to simmer, and cook 15 minutes or until noodles are tender.

# Potato-Meatloaf Meal

Meatloaf and potatoes; a match made in culinary heaven.

*Serves 8*

*Large Bag*

> 1 cup dehydrated shredded onions
> 2 cups dehydrated shredded potatoes (hash browns)
> 1 cup dehydrated sliced tomatoes

*Small Bag*

> 1 cup Italian Breadcrumbs (see page 24)
> 2 teaspoons beef bouillon
> 1 tablespoon powdered dehydrated tomato paste
> 1 tablespoon Meatloaf Seasoning (see page 22)

*To Store*

Place all ingredients into bags. Place small bag into large bag, seal, and label with cooking instructions.

*Cooking Ingredients*

> 2 pounds ground beef
> 4 cups water

*Directions*

1. Preheat oven to 350°F. Place ground beef into a large mixing bowl. Add water and stir until blended.
2. Add ingredients of small bag to ground beef and blend.
3. Add ingredients from large bag to ground beef, gently folding in.
4. Place into a greased, ovenproof, deep casserole dish and cover.
5. Place into preheated oven for 45 minutes. Remove cover, and place back in oven for an additional 15 minutes.

# Lemon, Chicken, and Kale Pasta

Packed with nutrients, this creamy pasta is a crowd pleaser.

*Serves 4*

*Large Bag*

> 2½ cups uncooked penne pasta
>
> 3 cups dehydrated kale

*Small Bag*

> 1 teaspoon garlic powder
>
> 2 teaspoons dehydrated lemon zest
>
> 1 teaspoon sea salt

*To Store*

Place all ingredients into bags. Place small bag into large bag, seal, and label with cooking instructions.

*Cooking Ingredients*

> 4½ cups water
>
> ½ cup ricotta cheese
>
> ½ cup Parmesan cheese
>
> 2 ounces cream cheese
>
> 3 boneless, skinless chicken breasts, cooked and shredded

*Directions*

1. Place water in a large sauté pan and bring to a boil. Pour ingredients from the large bag into water, cover, and let simmer over medium-low heat for 10 minutes.
2. In a separate bowl, combine the cheeses and contents of small bag and stir. Set aside.
3. Uncover pasta and add shredded chicken. Stir and let simmer for 1 to 2 minutes or until liquid is reduced.
4. Remove pan from heat and stir in cheese mixture until pasta is evenly coated. Serve hot.

# Mascarpone and Spinach Linguine

This refreshing pasta is a wonderful summer dish.

*Serves 6*

### Large Bag

> 5 cups dehydrated baby spinach
> 2 cups dehydrated halved cherry tomatoes

### Medium Bag

> 9 ounces linguine noodles, broken in half

### Small Bag

> 1½ teaspoons dehydrated lemon zest
> ½ teaspoon sea salt
> ½ teaspoon pepper
> ⅛ teaspoon nutmeg

### To Store

Place all ingredients into bags. Place smaller bags into large bag, seal, and label with cooking instructions.

### Cooking Ingredients

> 3 tablespoons cream cheese
> 1 cup mascarpone cheese
> 2 tablespoons grated Parmesan cheese

### Directions

1. Bring a large pot of water to a boil. Add the ingredients from the large and medium bags. Boil until pasta and tomatoes are tender, about 8 minutes.
2. Drain pasta water, reserving 1 cup of the drained water.
3. In a mixing bowl, add cream cheese, mascarpone cheese, and the contents of the small bag. Gently whisk the cheese mixture together while slowly adding the reserved pasta water until smooth and creamy. (Note: It may not be necessary to use all of the pasta water.)
4. Add the creamy cheese sauce to the pasta mixture and stir until completely coated. Sprinkle with Parmesan cheese. Serve hot.

*Top left moving clockwise:* Carrot, Corn, and Cherry Tomato Soup (page 75); Roasted Red Pepper and Gouda Soup (page 77); Mint Pea Soup (page 46); Spinach Soup (page 95); Portobello Soup (page 94)

*Top left moving clockwise:* Citrus and Dill Cheese Ball (page 36); Basil Pesto Dip (page 29); Kale and Garlic Hummus (page 35); Caramelized Onion, Squash, and Goat Cheese Turnovers (page 28)

*Top left moving clockwise:* Wasabi, Kale, Sesame Seed, Rice Rollups (page 198); Squash and Apple Rollup (page 198); Spiced Dehydrated Veggie Trail Mix (page 195); Kale Protein Shake (page 189); Veggie Omelette (page 196); Potato, Apple, Veggie Pancake (page 194); Spicy Bean Burrito (page 192)

*Top left moving clockwise:* Apricot and Rice (page 124), Apricot Chicken (page 98), Spanish Rice (page 69), Tabbouleh (page 118)

Veggie Strata (page 122)

*Top left moving clockwise:* Italian Spiral Veggies (page 121), Veggie and Hummus Stuffed Shells (page 114), Mascarpone and Spinach Linguine (page 112)

*Top left moving clockwise:* Banana Muffins (page 161); Jalapeño Corn Muffins (page 169); Blueberry Oatmeal Bars (page 150); Apple Raisin Cinnamon Roll Pie (page 152); Fruit Bowl Cookies (page 157); Pineapple, Coconut, Mango Dump Cake (page 142)

*Top left moving clockwise:* Blueberry Syrup (page 187), Spicy Sausage Breakfast Bake (page 183), Apricot Syrup (page 187)

# Veggie Burger

One-bag veggie burgers in a snap. Blend the dry ingredients in a blender before storing.

*Serves 4*

*Large Bag*

> 1½ cups dehydrated refried beans
> ½ cup dehydrated Kale and Garlic Hummus (see page 35)
> ½ cup dehydrated spinach
> ¼ cup dehydrated sliced tomato
> ½ cup dehydrated chopped yellow bell pepper
> ¼ cup dehydrated shredded onion

*To Store*

Place all dry ingredients into a blender and blend. Place blended ingredients into large bag, seal, and label with cooking instructions.

*Cooking Ingredients*

> 2 cups boiling water
> 2 tablespoons olive oil

*Directions*

1. Add boiling water to bag, stir until blended, add more water if needed, and let set until cooled and thickened.
2. Shape mixture into 4 patties. Heat a skillet over medium-high heat and add olive oil.
3. Cook patties 5 minutes on each side or until a crispy brown.

# Veggie and Hummus Stuffed Shells

Hummus is a delicious and nutritious alternative to cheese in these exciting stuffed shells.

*Serves 6*

### Large Bag

18 uncooked jumbo pasta shells

### Small Bag

1 cup Spicy Roasted Red Pepper Hummus (see page 33)
½ cup dehydrated parsley
¼ cup dehydrated diced onions

### To Store

Place all ingredients into bags. Place small bag into large bag, seal, and label with cooking instructions.

### Cooking Ingredients

2 cups warm water
2 cups ricotta cheese
2 eggs
1 (24-ounce) jar spaghetti sauce
2 cups mozzarella cheese

### Directions

1. Bring a large pot of water to a boil. Addn pasta shells from large bag, cook until tender, remove, and set aside.
2. Place ingredients from small bag into a mixing bowl. Add warm water, stir until blended, and let set 10 minutes.
3. Preheat oven to 350ºF. Add ricotta cheese and eggs to bowl, and blend until smooth.
4. Stuff each shell with mixture and place into a greased 9 x 13-inch baking dish.
5. Cover shells with spaghetti sauce. Sprinkle mozzarella cheese over top of shells.
6. Place in preheated oven, uncovered, for 25 to 30 minutes, until cheese is bubbly and golden brown.

# Loaded Veggie Turkey Meatloaf

An alternative to traditional meatloaf, packed with vegetables for the health-conscious family.

*Serves 8*

*Large Bag*

¼ cup dehydrated diced onion
¼ cup dehydrated shredded carrots
2 tablespoons dehydrated chopped red bell peppers
¼ cup dehydrated shredded zucchini
¼ cup dehydrated shredded squash

*Small Bag*

1 cup Italian Breadcrumbs (see page 24)
1 tablespoon Meatloaf Seasoning (see page 22)

*To Store*

Place all ingredients into bags. Place small bag into large bag, seal, and label with cooking instructions.

*Cooking Ingredients*

4 cups boiling water
1½ pounds ground turkey
1 egg
¼ cup Parmesan cheese
½ cup milk

*Directions*

1. Place ingredients from large bag in a bowl with boiling water, cover, and set aside for 15 to 20 minutes until veggies are tender and cooled. Lightly drain off excess water, but do not press or squeeze.
2. Preheat oven to 350°F.
3. In a separate bowl, mix together turkey, egg, cheese, and milk. Add ingredients from the small bag. Fold in hydrated veggies.
4. Place meatloaf into a 9 x 5-inch greased loaf pan. Bake, uncovered, for 1 hour and 15 minutes.

# Spiral Veggie Frittata

This colorful mix of thin spiraled veggies makes a delicious and beautiful side dish. (See page 12 for instructions on spiraling fruits and veggies.)

*Serves 6*

### Large Bag

    1 bird's nest dehydrated spiraled cucumber
    2 bird's nests dehydrated spiraled sweet potato
    2 bird's nests dehydrated spiraled onion
    2 bird's nests dehydrated spiraled turnip
    ¼ cup dehydrated chopped tomatoes

### Small Bag

    ½ teaspoon dehydrated crushed garlic cloves
    ½ teaspoon dehydrated chopped mint
    ½ teaspoon dehydrated chopped parsley
    ½ teaspoon dehydrated chopped dill
    ¼ teaspoon ground pepper

### To Store

Place all ingredients into bags. Place small bag into large bag, seal, and label with cooking instructions.

### Cooking Ingredients

    8 cups water
    1 tablespoon olive oil
    8 eggs, beaten
    ½ cup shredded mozzarella cheese

### Directions

1. Place ingredients from large bag with water in an ovenproof, nonstick skillet. Cover, bring to boil on top of stove, and reduce heat to simmer for 10 to 15 minutes (until hydrated). Drain water.
2. Toss in olive oil. Let cool until warm.
3. Preheat oven to 350°F. Place veggies into a greased 10 x 10-inch baking dish.
4. Add small bag of herbs to beaten eggs.

5. Pour egg mixture over hydrated spiraled veggies in baking dish.
6. Sprinkle with shredded mozzarella cheese.
7. Bake in preheated oven for 20 minutes, or until golden brown and knife comes out clean when inserted in center.

# Spiral Carrots with Coconut

Delicious carrots and coconut glazed with brown sugar and pecans. (See page 12 for instructions on spiraling fruits and veggies.)

*Serves 6*

### Large Bag

4 bird's nests dehydrated spiraled carrots
½ cup dehydrated coconut flakes

### Small Bag

½ cup chopped pecans
½ cup brown sugar

### To Store

Place all ingredients into bags. Place small bag into large bag, seal, and label with cooking instructions.

### Cooking Ingredients

6 cups water
1 tablespoon butter

### Directions

1. Place ingredients from large bag into a pot with water, cover, and bring to a boil. Reduce heat to simmer for 40 minutes or until carrots are tender.
2. Remove from heat, drain water, and add butter.
3. Add ingredients from small bag and gently toss in carrots and coconut.

# Tabbouleh

This Levantine vegetarian dish is more than just a salad.

*Serves 8*

### Large Bag

> 4 cups dehydrated parsley (do not crush)
> ½ cup dehydrated fresh mint, chopped
> ½ cup dehydrated chopped scallions
> ¼ teaspoon cumin
> 1 tablespoon finely crushed dehydrated lemon
> ¼ teaspoon ground pepper
> ½ teaspoon Vinegar Powder (see page 6)

### Medium Bag

> 2½ cups dehydrated halved cherry tomatoes
> 1½ cups bulgur wheat

### To Store

Place all ingredients into bags. Place medium bag into large bag, seal, and label with cooking instructions.

### Cooking Ingredients

> 6¼ cups water, divided
> ¼ cup olive oil

### Directions

1. Place ingredients from medium bag into pot, add 6 cups water, and stir.
2. Bring to boil, cover, reduce heat to low, and cook 15 minutes. Turn off heat. Do not drain excess water.
3. Fold ingredients from large bag into pot.
4. Add an additional ¼ cup water if needed.
5. Place cover back on pot and let set 10 minutes.
6. Fold in oil.

# Apple Stuffing

Enhance your stuffing with the beautiful sweetness of apples.

*Serves 6*

### Large Bag

> 6 cups dehydrated bread cubes
> 2 teaspoons sage

### Medium Bag

> 2 cups dehydrated shredded apples
> ¼ cup dehydrated shredded onions
> 1 cup dehydrated shredded zucchini

### To Store

Place all ingredients into bags. Place smaller bag into large bag, seal, and label with cooking instructions.

### Cooking Ingredients

> 5 cups water
> 3 tablespoons butter

### Directions

1. Place ingredients from medium bag into a pot.
2. Add water and butter, bring to a boil, cover, and reduce heat to simmer 10 minutes.
3. Fold ingredients from large bag into pot. Continue mixing until bread cubes are soft. Add extra water if needed.
4. Stuff a chicken, turkey, or pork before roasting, or simply place stuffing into a greased 10 x 10-inch baking dish and bake for 30 minutes in preheated oven at 350ºF.

# Cheesy Spiral Apple-Potato Bake

Just add water to this cheesy potato and apple dish. (See page 12 for instructions on spiraling fruits and veggies.)

*Serves 8*

*Large Bag*

   6 bird's nests dehydrated spiraled potatoes or 6 cups dehydrated hash browns
   3 bird's nests dehydrated spiraled apples
   1 cup dehydrated shredded sweet onion
   ½ cup dehydrated corn

*Small Bag*

   1½ cups powdered cheese
   ½ cup powdered nonfat milk
   2 teaspoons cornstarch

*To Store*

Place all ingredients into bags. Place smaller bag into large bag, seal, and label with cooking instructions.

*Cooking Ingredients*

   8 cups boiling water
   2 cups water

*Directions*

1. Grease a deep 9 x 12-inch casserole dish. Place ingredients from large bag into bottom of the dish.
2. Pour boiling water over top of the dehydrated ingredients, cover, and let set 20 minutes until cooled (do not drain water after cooling).
3. Preheat oven to 350°F. Place ingredients from small bag into a blender with 2 cups water, blend until smooth, pour over ingredients in casserole dish, and cover.
4. Place casserole into preheated oven and bake for 45 minutes. Remove cover and place back in oven for an additional 15 minutes until top is golden brown.

# Italian Spiral Veggies

Quick and easy pasta and veggies. (See page 12 for instructions on spiraling fruits and veggies.)

*Serves 8*

*Large Bag*

> 2 bird's nests dehydrated zucchini
> 2 bird's nests dehydrated summer squash
> 2 cups penne pasta

*Small Bag*

> 2 tablespoons Italian Seasoning (see page 19)

*To Store*

Place all ingredients into bags. Place small bag into large bag, seal, and label with cooking instructions.

*Cooking Ingredients*

> 1 tablespoon olive oil

*Directions*

1. Bring a large pot of water to a boil. Place ingredients from large bag into pot of boiling water, cook until tender, approximately 10 minutes, and drain water.
2. Add olive oil to pasta and spiral vegetables.
3. Add seasoning from small bag into pasta and spiral vegetables, and toss until well blended.
4. Cover and let set for 5 minutes before serving.

# Veggie Strata

This easy vegetable side dish is perfect for large family gatherings.

*Serves 8*

### Large Bag

1 cup dehydrated ½-inch strips red bell pepper
1 bird's nest dehydrated spiraled zucchini
1 bird's nest dehydrated sliced summer squash
½ cup dehydrated sliced mushrooms
1 cup dehydrated shredded onion
1 cup dehydrated ½-inch strips yellow bell pepper

### Medium Bag

4 cups dehydrated bread cubes

### To Store

Place all ingredients into bags. Place medium bag into large bag, seal, and label with cooking instructions.

### Cooking Ingredients

8 cups boiling water
8 eggs
8 ounces cream cheese, softened
½ cup half-and-half

### Directions

1. Place ingredients from large bag into a mixing bowl.
2. Add boiling water, cover, let set 10 to 15 minutes until water is lukewarm, and drain.
3. Add ingredients from medium bag to hydrated veggies and gently toss together. Generously grease a deep, 10- to 12-inch pan and place veggies in it.
4. Preheat oven to 325°F. In a separate bowl, beat eggs, cream cheese, and half-and-half until smooth. Pour batter over bread cubes and veggies.
5. Place pan in preheated oven and bake for 1 hour or until the strata puffs up and turns golden brown.

# Mushroom Couscous

Such a simple and easy side dish, filled with mushrooms and ready in just 5 minutes.

*Serves 4*

### Large Bag

- 1 cup uncooked couscous
- 1 cup dehydrated sliced mushrooms
- 1 tablespoon dehydrated parsley
- 2 teaspoons chicken bouillon

### To Store

Place all ingredients into large bag, seal, and label with cooking instructions.

### Cooking Ingredients

- 2 cups water
- 1 tablespoon butter

### Directions

1. Place ingredients from large bag into a pot. Add water and butter.
2. Bring to a boil, cover, and reduce heat to simmer for 5 minutes.

# Apricot and Rice

Just add water for this excellent side dish. Served well under your fish, chicken, or turkey.

*Serves 6*

*Large Bag*

>   2 cups uncooked white rice
>   1 tablespoon chicken bouillon
>   ½ teaspoon dried thyme
>   ½ teaspoon marjoram
>   ⅓ cup sliced almonds

*Small Bag*

>   1 cup dehydrated chopped apricots
>   ¼ cup dehydrated chopped onions
>   ¼ cup dehydrated chopped red bell peppers

*To Store*

Place all ingredients into bags. Place small bag into large bag, seal, and label with cooking instructions.

*Cooking Ingredients*

>   5 cups water

*Directions*

1.  Place ingredients from large and small bags into a pot.
2.  Add water, bring to a boil, cover, reduce heat to a simmer, and cook 25 minutes or until rice is tender and water is absorbed.

# Stuffing with Cranberries

Fast and easy. Delicious served with poultry, pork, or fish.

*Serves 4*

*Large Bag*

> 4 cups dehydrated ½-inch bread cubes

*Small Bag*

> ½ cup dehydrated cranberries
> 2 teaspoons poultry seasoning
> ¼ cup dehydrated chopped onions
> ½ tablespoon dehydrated chopped celery
> ½ tablespoon dehydrated parsley

*To Store*

Place all ingredients into bags. Place small bag into large bag, seal, and label with cooking instructions.

*Cooking Ingredients*

> 3 cups water
> 2 tablespoons butter

*Directions*

1. Place ingredients from small bag into a pot. Add water and butter, bring to a boil for 1 minute, cover, remove from heat, and let set 5 minutes.
2. Place dehydrated bread cubes from large bag into the pot, and gently fold in until bread is covered and moist. Keep covered until ready to serve.
3. As an optional finishing touch, place stuffing into a preheated oven at 400 F°, and broil on low to brown the top for that extra crunch.

# Veggie-Loaded Mashed Potato Bake

If you love mashed potatoes, then this recipe does not disappoint.

*Serves 8*

*Large Bag*

>    2 cups dehydrated baby spinach
>    2 cups dehydrated sliced tomatoes
>    2 cups dehydrated sliced mushrooms

*Medium Bag*

>    3 cups instant mashed potatoes

*Small Bag*

>    1 cup powdered cheese
>    6 tablespoons powdered nonfat milk
>    1 tablespoon cornstarch

*To Store*

Place all ingredients into bags. Place smaller bags into large bag, seal, and label with cooking instructions.

*Cooking Ingredients*

>    1 cup boiling water
>    2 tablespoons butter
>    8 cups warm water
>    3 eggs

*Directions*

1.  Place ingredients from medium bag into a bowl. Add 1 cup boiling water and butter. Gently stir with a fork, set aside, and let cool.
2.  Preheat oven to 375°F. Place ingredients from small bag into a blender with 8 cups warm water and blend until smooth.
3.  Place ingredients from large bag into a 9 x 13-inch greased baking dish.
4.  Pour mixture from blender over dehydrated vegetables in baking dish.
5.  Add eggs to cooled mashed potatoes, stir until blended well, and layer over veggies and cheese.
6.  Place into preheated oven and bake for 35 to 40 minutes until top is a crispy golden brown.

# Eggplant Bake

Delicious veggies layered with sauce and cheese. Add some of your seasoned bread-crumbs for that extra crunch.

*Serves 6*

*Large Bag*

> 6 cups dehydrated sliced eggplant
> 3 cups dehydrated sliced tomatoes
> 2 cups dehydrated shredded onions
> 2 cups dehydrated sliced mushrooms
> 1 cup seasoned breadcrumbs (optional)

*To Store*

Place all ingredients into large bag, seal, and label with cooking instructions.

*Cooking Ingredients*

> 6 cups water
> 1 (24-ounce) jar marinara sauce
> 2½ cups shredded mozzarella cheese

*Directions*

1. Preheat oven to 350°F. Place ingredients from large bag into a deep baking dish. Add water and marinara sauce. Cover and place in a preheated oven.
2. Bake for 40 minutes.
3. Remove cover. Sprinkle shredded mozzarella cheese over eggplant, and return to oven for another 20 minutes or until golden brown.

# Cheesy Cabbage Bake

Just add water to this easy side dish. Pairs excellently with ham or kielbasa.

*Serves 8*

*Large Bag*

> 6 cups dehydrated shredded cabbage
> 1 cup dehydrated shredded onions
> 1 cup dehydrated sliced tomatoes

*Small Bag*

> ½ cup powdered cheese
> ½ cup powdered milk
> 1 teaspoon powdered garlic

*To Store*

Place all ingredients into bags. Place small bag into large bag, seal, and label with cooking instructions.

*Cooking Ingredients*

> 9 cups warm water

*Directions*

1. Preheat oven to 350ºF. Place ingredients from large bag into a deep casserole dish. Set aside.
2. Place ingredients in a small bag into blender with warm water. Blend until smooth.
3. Pour ingredients from blender over top the of ingredients in casserole dish. Cover casserole dish.
4. Place into preheated oven and bake for 45 minutes. Remove cover and place back in the oven for an additional 15 minutes.

# Tomato and Onion Bake

A tomato lover's dish.

*Serves 8*

## Large Bag

    3 cups dehydrated sliced tomatoes
    2 cups dehydrated halved cherry tomatoes
    ¼ cup dehydrated parsley
    ½ cup dehydrated shredded onion

## Medium Bag

    4 cups dehydrated ½-inch bread cubes

## To Store

Place all ingredients into bags. Place small bag into large bag, seal, and label with cooking instructions.

## Cooking Ingredients

    7 cups water
    2 tablespoons olive oil
    2 cups shredded mozzarella cheese

## Directions

1. Preheat oven to 350ºF. Place ingredients from large bag into a pot with water, cover, bring to boil, and reduce heat to simmer for 10 minutes. Do not drain water. Pour into a 10 x 10-inch greased baking dish.
2. Open medium bag, add olive oil to bag, shake for 1 minute, and sprinkle bread cubes over tomato mixture.
3. Sprinkle mozzarella over top of bread cubes and tomatoes.
4. Place in preheated oven for 30 to 35 minutes or until cheese is melted, bubbling, and golden brown.

# Barley, Corn, and Black Bean Cheese Bake

Just add water to complete this cheesy baked casserole.

*Serves 10*

*Large Bag*

> 1 cup quick-cooking barley
> ½ cup bulgur
> ½ cup dehydrated corn
> ½ cup dehydrated shredded carrots
> ⅓ cup dehydrated parsley
> ¼ cup dehydrated chopped onion
> 1 cup dry black beans

*Small Bag*

> 1 cup powdered cheese
> 3 tablespoons nonfat milk
> 3 teaspoons vegetable bouillon

*To Store*

Place all ingredients into bags. Place small bag into large bag, seal, and label with cooking instructions.

*Cooking Ingredients*

> 10½ cups water

*Directions*

1. Preheat oven to 350ºF.
2. Place ingredients from large and small bags into a 6-quart Dutch oven.
3. Add water, stir, and cover.
4. Place into preheated oven for 60 minutes or until top of veggies is golden brown.

# Baked Corn with Peppers and Onions

Delicious country-style corn casserole.

*Serves 8*

*Large Bag*

> 2 cups dehydrated corn
> ½ cup dehydrated chopped red bell pepper
> ½ cup dehydrated shredded onion

*Small Bag*

> 6 tablespoons powdered nonfat milk
> 1 tablespoon sugar
> 1 tablespoon cornstarch

*To Store*

Place all ingredients into bags. Place small bag into large bag, seal, and label with cooking instructions.

*Cooking Ingredients*

> 9 cups warm water, divided
> 3 eggs
> 3 tablespoons butter, softened
> 1 cup Chile and Lime Breadcrumbs (see page 26) (optional)

*Directions*

1. Place ingredients from large bag into a 3-quart greased Dutch oven.
2. Add 7 cups boiling water, cover, and let set until cooled (about 30 minutes).
3. Preheat oven to 350°F.
4. Place ingredients from small bag into a blender. Add 2 cups warm water, eggs, and butter and blend until smooth.
5. Pour mixture from blender over top of corn in Dutch oven.
6. Sprinkle breadcrumbs over top of corn, if desired.
7. Cover dish and place into preheated oven. Bake 45 minutes, remove cover, and place back into oven for 15 minutes until golden brown.

# Spinach Bake

A healthy and vibrant side dish.

*Serves 6*

*Large Bag*

>    4 cups dehydrated spinach, crushed
>    ¼ cup dehydrated shredded onion
>    ½ teaspoon crushed dehydrated basil
>    1 teaspoon fennel seed
>    1 cup dehydrated sliced mushrooms
>    2 tablespoons powdered dehydrated tomato paste

*Small Bag*

>    3 tablespoons powdered nonfat milk
>    ½ teaspoon salt
>    1 teaspoon baking powder
>    1½ cups flour
>    ½ cup powdered cheese

*To Store*

Place all ingredients into bags. Place small bag into large bag, seal, and label with cooking instructions.

*Cooking Ingredients*

>    6½ cups water
>    2 eggs

*Directions*

1. Preheat oven to 350°F.
2. Place ingredients from small bag into a blender with water and eggs. Blend until smooth.
3. Pour ingredients from large bag into a greased, deep 10 x 10-inch casserole dish.
4. Pour batter from blender over top of spinach mixture.
5. Place in preheated oven for 25 to 30 minutes until top has formed a crust that is golden brown.

# Falafel Patties

It's so simple and easy to make this Middle Eastern favorite.

*Makes 8 patties*

## Large Bag

    1 cup powdered dehydrated chickpeas
    ¼ cup all-purpose flour
    ¼ cup dehydrated parsley
    2 tablespoons sesame seeds
    1 teaspoon cumin
    1 teaspoon baking powder
    1 teaspoon dehydrated lemon zest
    ½ teaspoon powdered garlic

## To Store

Place all ingredients into large bag, seal, and label with cooking instructions.

## Cooking Ingredients

    1½ cups warm water
    4 tablespoons olive oil
    Plain yogurt (optional)

## Directions

1. Place ingredients from large bag into a blender with warm water, blend, and let set 15 minutes until thickened. Texture should be easy to shape into 1½-inch round balls. If too dry, add another tablespoon of water.
2. Heat frying pan with olive oil.
4. Press each ball into the heated pan to shape patties.
5. Cook 4 minutes on each side.
6. Serve with a dollop of yogurt, if desired.

# Mushroom Barley with Dill

Dill brings an aromatic and flavorful undertone to this wholesome dish.

*Serves 6*

*Large Bag*

> 1 cup quick-cooking barley
> 1 cup dehydrated sliced mushrooms
> 2 tablespoons Spinach & Dill Seasoning (see page 20)

*To Store*

Place all ingredients into large bag, seal, and label with cooking instructions.

*Cooking Ingredients*

> 3 cups water

*Directions*

1. Place ingredients from large bag into a pot.
2. Add water, cover, bring to a boil, reduce heat, and simmer 30 minutes.

# Shredded Veggie Bake

A wonderful vegetarian casserole packed with all your favorites.

*Serves 6*

### Large Bag

 2 cups dehydrated shredded potatoes
 ¼ cup dehydrated shredded onions
 ¼ cup dehydrated shredded sweet red peppers
 ½ cup dehydrated shredded carrots
 ½ cup dehydrated shredded summer squash
 ½ cup dehydrated shredded zucchini

### To Store

Place all ingredients into large bag, seal, and label with cooking instructions.

### Cooking Ingredients

 2 cups shredded cheddar cheese blend
 ½ cup milk
 6½ cups boiling water

### Directions

1. Place ingredients from large bag in a mixing bowl. Add boiling water, cover, and let soak 20 minutes (do not drain water).
2. Add shredded cheese and milk.
3. Preheat oven to 350ºF. Place mixture in a greased 8 x 8-inch baking dish.
4. Place dish in preheated oven, uncovered, and bake 35 minutes until bubbling and golden brown.
5. Let cool 10 minutes and serve.

# Potato, Artichoke, and Goat Cheese Bake

The richness of goat cheese truly brings together the flavors in this instant family favorite.

*Serves 6*

*Large Bag*

> 2 cups dehydrated sliced potatoes
> ¼ cup dehydrated chopped leek
> ¾ cup dehydrated sliced artichoke hearts

*Small Bag*

> 1 cup dehydrated ½-inch bread cubes

*To Store*

Place all ingredients into bags. Place small bag into large bag, seal, and label with cooking instructions.

*Cooking Ingredients*

> 6 cups boiling water
> 1 cup heavy cream
> 6 ounces Parmesan cheese, grated
> 6 ounces goat cheese, crumbled
> 1 tablespoon melted butter

*Directions*

1. Place ingredients from large bag into an 8 x 10-inch baking dish with boiling water, cover, and let set 20 minutes (do not drain water).
2. Preheat oven to 400°F.
3. Mix together cream and Parmesan cheese, and pour over veggies. Top with goat cheese.
4. Mix bread cubes with melted butter. Layer on top.
5. Cover and place in preheated oven. Bake 25 to 30 minutes. Remove cover and bake an additional 10 minutes until golden brown.

# Apple, Cranberry, and Pecan Rice Dish

A sweet and unique side dish, rich with flavor.

*Serves 6*

*Large Bag*

>  2 cups uncooked white rice

*Medium Bag*

>  2 cups crumbled dehydrated sliced apples
>  ½ cup dehydrated cranberries
>  ¼ cup dehydrated chopped onions

*Small Bag*

>  1 tablespoon Citrus & Dill Seasoning (see page 16)
>  ½ cup chopped pecans

*To Store*

Place all ingredients into bags. Place small bag into large bag, seal, and label with cooking instructions.

*Cooking Ingredients*

>  6½ cups water

*Directions*

1. Place ingredients from large and medium bags into a pot.
2. Add water, bring to a boil, cover, reduce heat to simmer, and cook 20 to 25 minutes.
3. Fold ingredients from small bag containing spice and pecans into rice. Cover, let set a few minutes, and serve.

# Mango, Banana, and Raisin Quinoa

The light summertime flavors of mango and banana are a perfect complement to the earthiness of quinoa.

*Serves 6*

### Large Bag

   2 cups quinoa

### Medium Bag

   1 cup dehydrated sliced mango, cut into small pieces with kitchen scissors
   1 cup dehydrated sliced apples, cut into halves
   1 cup dehydrated sliced bananas
   1 slice dehydrated lemon, crushed

### Small Bag

   2 tablespoons dehydrated mint, crushed
   1 cup chopped pecans
   2 teaspoons cinnamon

### To Store

Place all ingredients into bags. Place smaller bags into large bag, seal, and label with cooking instructions.

### Cooking Ingredients

   6½ cups water
   2 tablespoons maple syrup (optional)

### Directions

1. Place ingredients from large and medium bags into a pot.
2. Add water, bring to a boil, reduce heat to simmer, and cook 15 minutes.
3. Fold in ingredients from small bag. Cover and let set for 2 minutes.
4. Drizzle each serving with maple syrup if desired.

# Tofu, Vegetables, and Ginger

The mild flavor of tofu contrasts well with the hot tanginess of ginger from the Sweet Asian Spice in this dish. Just add water and serve over rice. Tofu is a great protein substitute that can be easily dehydrated.

*Serves 4*

*Large Bag*

>   1 cup dehydrated 2-inch-cubed tofu
>   ¼ cup dehydrated chopped bell pepper
>   1 cup dehydrated chopped portobello mushrooms
>   ½ cup dehydrated snap peas
>   1 cup dehydrated shredded onion

*Small Bag*

>   1 tablespoon crushed dehydrated lemon slices
>   2 tablespoons dehydrated cilantro, crushed
>   2 tablespoons Sweet Asian Spice (see page 24)

*To Store*

Place all ingredients into bags. Place small bag into large bag, seal, and label with cooking instructions.

*Cooking Ingredients*

>   7 cups water

*Directions*

1. Place ingredients from large bag into a pot. Add water, bring to a boil, and reduce to simmer for 1 hour. Drain excess liquid.
2. Stir ingredients from small bag into pot, cover, and let set a few minutes.
3. Serve over cooked rice.

# Garden Parmesan Casserole

All your favorite veggies in one crunchy, saucy dish.

*Serves 6*

### Large Bag

2½ cups dehydrated sliced tomatoes
1 cup dehydrated halved cherry tomatoes
2 cups dehydrated sliced eggplant
½ cup dehydrated parsley
1 cup dehydrated sliced mushrooms
1 cup dehydrated sliced zucchini

### To Store

Place all ingredients into large bag, seal, and label with cooking instructions.

### Cooking Ingredients

8 cups boiling water
1 (24-ounce) jar marinara sauce
2 cups shredded mozzarella cheese
1 cup Italian Breadcrumbs (see page 24) (optional)

### Directions

1. Place ingredients from large bag into a Dutch oven or deep casserole dish. Add boiling water, cover, and let set 20 minutes or until cooled.
2. Preheat oven to 350°F.
3. Pour marinara sauce over the top of the casserole. Sprinkle with mozzarella cheese, and sprinkle breadcrumbs over cheese if desired.
4. Place in preheated oven for 45 minutes until golden brown and bubbling.

# Chapter 8

# Desserts in a Bag

If you're like us, you jumped straight to this chapter first. Don't think we would forget about our friends with a sweet tooth. There are endless dessert possibilities with dehydrated foods! Why buy instant cake and dessert mixes when you can make your own special creations? Have fun with the kids designing delicious dessert projects! You'll even save money!

# Pineapple, Coconut, Mango Dump Cake

Quick and easy tropical cake. True to its name, the "dump cake" means to dump all your ingredients into one bowl and stir.

*Serves 12*

### Large Bag

> 2½ cups all-purpose flour
> 1½ cups sugar
> 3½ teaspoons baking powder
> 1½ teaspoons baking soda
> ¼ teaspoon salt

### Small Bag

> 1 cup dehydrated pineapple tidbits
> ½ cup dehydrated coconut flakes, blended or crushed
> 1 cup dehydrated sliced mango, cut into 1 inch pieces

### To Store

Sift together ingredients for large bag. Place all ingredients into bags. Place small bag into large bag, seal, and label with cooking instructions.

### Cooking Ingredients

> 4 cups boiling water
> ½ cup cooking oil
> 3 eggs

### Directions

1. Place ingredients from small bag into mixing bowl. Add boiling water and let set until cooled (do not drain excess water).
2. Place ingredients from large bag into bowl; add oil and eggs. Mix until smooth.
3. Preheat oven to 350ºF. Pour mixture into 9 x 13-inch greased baking dish.
4. Place into preheated oven for 40 to 45 minutes or until golden brown and knife comes out clean when inserted in middle.

# Strawberry-Rhubarb Dump Cake

The sweetness of strawberry and the tartness of rhubarb, together in a no-fuss dump cake.

*Serves 12*

## Large Bag

> 2½ cups all-purpose flour
> 1½ cups sugar
> 3½ teaspoons baking powder
> 1½ teaspoons baking soda
> ¼ teaspoon salt

## Small Bag

> ½ cup dehydrated chopped rhubarb
> 2 cups dehydrated sliced strawberries
> 1 tablespoon cornstarch
> 1 tablespoon sugar

## To Store

Sift together ingredients for large bag. Place all ingredients into bags. Place small bag into large bag, seal, and label with cooking instructions.

## Cooking Ingredients

> 4 cups water, divided
> ½ cup cooking oil
> 3 eggs

## Directions

1. Place ingredients from small bag into a pot with 3 cups water, bring to a boil, stir until thickened, set aside, and let cool.
2. Preheat oven to 350°F.
3. Place ingredients from large bag into mixing bowl. Add 1 cup water, oil, and eggs. Mix until smooth, and pour batter into 9 x 13-inch greased baking dish.
4. Dump and swirl strawberry-rhubarb filling into batter.
5. Place cake into preheated oven for 40 to 45 minutes or until golden brown and a knife comes out clean when inserted in middle.

# Peach Dump Cake

The fastest way to visit Georgia.

*Serves 12*

*Large Bag*

> 2½ cups all-purpose flour
> 1½ cups sugar
> 3½ teaspoons baking powder
> ½ teaspoon baking soda
> ¼ teaspoon salt

*Small Bag*

> 2 cups dehydrated sliced peaches, cut in halves

*To Store*

Sift together ingredients for large bag. Place all ingredients into bags. Place small bag into large bag, seal, and label with cooking instructions.

*Cooking Ingredients*

> 3 eggs
> 4 cups water
> ½ cup cooking oil

*Directions*

1. Place ingredients from large and small bags into a mixing bowl. Add eggs, water and cooking oil. Mix until smooth; mixture should be loose.
2. Cover and let set 15 minutes.
3. Preheat oven to 350°F. Pour batter into a greased 9 x 13-inch baking dish.
4. Place dish into preheated oven for 40 to 45 minutes or until golden brown and a knife comes out clean when inserted in middle.

# Apple-Raisin Dump Cake

Crisp apples and gooey raisins together in a simple-to-make cake.

*Serves 12*

*Large Bag*

2½ cups all-purpose flour

1½ cups sugar

3½ teaspoons baking powder

½ teaspoon baking soda

¼ teaspoon salt

*Medium Bag*

4 cups dehydrated sliced apples, cut into thirds

⅔ cup raisins

½ cup brown sugar

½ cup granulated sugar

3 tablespoons cornstarch

1 tablespoon apple pie spice

*To Store*

Sift together ingredients for large bag. Place all ingredients into bags. Place medium bag into large bag, seal, and label with cooking instructions.

*Cooking Ingredients*

7½ cups water, divided

3 eggs

½ cup cooking oil

*Directions*

1. Place ingredients from medium bag into a pot. Add 6 cups water, stir. Bring to a boil, reduce heat to simmer, and stir 10 minutes or until thickened. Remove from heat and let cool.
2. Preheat oven to 350°F.
3. Add ingredients from large bag into a mixing bowl. Add 1½ cups water, eggs, and oil and blend until a smooth batter.
4. Pour apple filling into a greased 9 x 13-inch baking dish. Pour batter over top of filling.
5. Place cake in preheated oven for 40 to 45 minutes or until batter has risen and turns golden brown.
6. Scoop out with large spoon and serve hot.

# Gluten-Free Loaded Fruitcake

This is a healthy and delicious gluten-free option for dessert.

*Serves 6*

*Large Bag*

 ½ cup cornmeal
 ¾ cup millet flour
 ⅔ cup sugar
 ½ teaspoon baking powder
 ¼ teaspoon baking soda
 3 tablespoons nonfat powdered milk

*Small Bag*

 2 tablespoons dehydrated sliced strawberries, crushed
 2 tablespoons dehydrated sliced peaches, cut into small bits
 2 tablespoons dehydrated crushed pineapple
 2 tablespoons dehydrated sliced bananas, cut into bits

*To Store*

Place all ingredients into bags. Place small bag into large bag, seal, and label with cooking instructions.

*Cooking Ingredients*

 1½ cups boiling water
 2 eggs
 ¼ cup cooking oil
 ¾ cup water

*Directions*

1. Place ingredients from small bag into a bowl with boiling water, cover, and let set until cool. Lightly drain off excess water (do not press or squeeze).
2. Preheat oven to 325°F.
3. Place ingredients from large bag into mixing bowl, add eggs, oil, and water, and blend until a smooth batter. Then, fold in hydrated drained fruit.
4. Pour batter into a greased 10-inch round cake pan.
5. Place cake into preheated oven for 30 minutes or until golden brown and it springs back in middle when touched.

# Blueberry Bundt Cake

A sweet and decadent treat without hassle.

*Serves 12*

*Large Bag*

>   3 cups cake flour
>   1¾ cups sugar
>   3 teaspoons baking powder
>   ¼ teaspoon salt
>   1 tablespoon dehydrated lemon zest

*Small Bag*

>   2 cups dehydrated blueberries
>   1 tablespoon sugar
>   1 tablespoon cornstarch

*To Store*

Place all ingredients into bags. Place small bag into large bag, seal, and label with cooking instructions.

*Cooking Ingredients*

>   3 cups water, divided
>   4 eggs
>   1½ sticks (¾ cup) butter, softened

*Directions*

1. Place ingredients from small bag into a saucepan. Add 2 cups water, bring to a boil, reduce to simmer, and cook until thickened. Remove from heat and let set until cooled and hydrated.
2. Preheat oven to 350°F.
3. Place ingredients from large bag into a mixing bowl. Add eggs, butter, and 1 cup water. Blend until a smooth batter.
4. Pour batter into a greased Bundt pan, then spoon the cooled blueberries on top. Bake 50 to 55 minutes until golden brown and knife comes out clean when inserted.

# Quick Crunchy Cranberry Cake

Cranberries and walnuts create a burst of sweetness with a crunch in this delicious dessert.

*Serves 8*

### Large Bag

> 1½ cups flour
> 1 cup sugar
> 2 teaspoons baking powder
> ½ teaspoon salt
> ¼ cup powdered milk

### Small Bag

> 1 cup dehydrated cranberries
> ¾ cup brown sugar
> ½ cup chopped walnuts

### To Store

Place all ingredients into bags. Place small bag into large bag, seal, and label with cooking instructions.

### Cooking Ingredients

> 1 cup water
> ½ stick butter (¼ cup), softened
> 3 eggs

### Directions

1. Preheat oven to 350ºF. Place ingredients from large bag in a mixing bowl with water, butter, and eggs. Mix until smooth.
2. Add ingredients from small bag by lightly folding or swirling (do not blend) into batter.
3. Pour batter into a greased 9 x 13-inch baking dish. Bake in preheated oven for 20 to 25 minutes or until a knife inserted in center comes out clean.

# Pumpkin Pie Crisp Rice Treats

A delicious twist to a classic treat! This will be an instant hit in the autumn, spring-time, night time, bath time . . . whenever and wherever!

*Serves 12*

*Large Bag*

> 6 cups puffed rice cereal

*Medium Bag*

> 4 cups marshmallows

*Small Bag*

> 1 tablespoon powdered dehydrated pumpkin
> 2 teaspoons Pumpkin Pie Spice (see page 23)

*To Store*

Place all ingredients into bags. Place smaller bags into large bag, seal, and label with cooking instructions.

*Cooking Ingredients*

> 3 tablespoons butter
> ½ cup water
> ¼ teaspoon vanilla extract
> Pumpkin seeds for garnish (optional)

*Directions*

1. In a skillet over low heat, add butter, water, and vanilla and heat until melted.
2. Add ingredients from small bag to skillet and simmer on low for 10 to 15 minutes, stirring frequently.
3. Add marshmallows from medium bag to mixture. Stir constantly until melted and well blended.
4. Add rice cereal from large bag, folding into mixture until completely coated. Pour into greased 9 x 13-inch baking pan. Lightly flatten. Chill in the refrigerator for 30 minutes. Cut into 2-inch squares.
5. Garnish with pumpkin seeds if desired.

# Blueberry Oatmeal Bars

A sweet treat for breakfast or dessert.

*Makes 12 bars*

### Large Bag

> 1⅓ cups all-purpose flour
> ¼ teaspoon baking soda
> ¼ teaspoon salt
> 1 cup rolled oats
> ½ cup brown sugar

### Small Bag

> 1 cup dehydrated blueberries
> 1 teaspoon dehydrated lemon zest
> 1 tablespoon cornstarch

### To Store

Place all ingredients into bags. Place small bag into large bag, seal, and label with cooking instructions.

### Cooking Ingredients

> 6 ounces cream cheese, softened
> 3 cups water

### Directions

1. Place ingredients from large bag into mixing bowl, stir, and fold in softened cream cheese until batter is crumbly.
2. Reserving 1 cup for topping, press remaining crumb batter into a 10 x 10-inch greased baking pan.
3. Place ingredients from small bag into a pot. Add water, bring to a boil, and stir constantly until thickened and hydrated. Set aside to cool.
4. Preheat oven to 350ºF. When filling is cooled, spread evenly over batter in pan.
5. Sprinkle reserved crumb batter over filling. Place pan in preheated oven and bake for 35 minutes.
6. Cool, cut into 12 bars, and refrigerate.

# Peach, Raisin, and Oatmeal Cookies

Add some extra sweetness to your oatmeal cookies.

*Makes 2½ dozen*

### Large Bag
  1½ cups brown sugar
  1 cup flour
  3½ cups rolled oats
  1 teaspoon salt
  ½ teaspoon baking soda

### Small Bag
  1 cup dehydrated sliced peaches (cut into thirds)
  1 cup raisins

### To Store
Place all ingredients into bags. Place small bag into large bag, seal, and label with cooking instructions.

### Cooking Ingredients
  2 cups boiling water
  2 sticks butter, softened
  1 egg
  ¼ cup water

### Directions
1. Place ingredients from small bag into a bowl. Add 2 cups boiling water. Let set while preparing batter.
2. Place ingredients from large bag into a separate mixing bowl. Add butter, egg, and ¼ cup water, and mix to a smooth batter.
3. Lightly drain extra water from peaches and raisins (do not press or squeeze out water). Fold fruit into batter.
4. Grease baking pan. Drop 1 tablespoon of batter per cookie onto baking pan.
5. Bake 15 to 18 minutes until golden brown.

# Apple-Raisin Cinnamon Roll Pie

A classic spicy and sweet autumn treat to satisfy your cravings.

*Serves 8*

### Large Bag

    4 cups dehydrated sliced apples, cut into thirds
    ⅔ cup raisins
    1 cup sugar
    3 tablespoons cornstarch
    1 tablespoon apple pie spice

### To Store

Place all ingredients into large bag, seal, and label with cooking instructions.

### Cooking Ingredients

    6 cups water
    1 package uncooked, refrigerated cinnamon rolls with frosting

### Directions

1. Place ingredients from large bag into a pot. Add water, stir, bring to a boil, reduce heat to simmer, stir, cover, and simmer 10 minutes until thickened.
2. Preheat oven to 350°F. Remove cinnamon rolls from the package. Place them together, roll them out flat with rolling pin, and place into a greased 9 x 13-inch pan.
3. Pour apple and raisin mixture over top of cinnamon rolls.
4. Place pan into preheated oven for 25 minutes.
5. Drizzle frosting from package over apples and raisins.

# Apple-Raisin Custard Bake

Moist and delicious custard over baked apples.

*Serves 8*

*Large Bag*

> 4 cups dehydrated thinly sliced apples
> 1 cup raisins
> ½ cup brown sugar
> 1 teaspoon cinnamon

*Small Bag*

> 1½ cups all-purpose flour
> ½ teaspoon salt
> 2 tablespoons sugar

*To Store*

Place all ingredients into bags. Place small bag into large bag, seal, and label with cooking instructions.

*Cooking Ingredients*

> 2 cups boiling water
> ¼ stick (⅛ cup) butter, softened
> 1½ cups milk
> 6 eggs

*Directions*

1. Place ingredients from large bag into a bowl with boiling water and butter. Cover, and let set 10 to 15 minutes until cooled and hydrated.
2. Preheat oven to 400°F.
3. Pour hydrated apple mixture into bottom of greased 9 x 13-inch baking dish.
4. Blend ingredients from small bag with milk and eggs until smooth. Pour over apples and raisins.
5. Place pan into preheated oven for 20 to 25 minutes until golden brown and a knife inserted in center comes out clean.

# Apple-Cranberry Turnovers

Apples and cranberries make up this delicious and colorful easy-to-eat dessert

*Serves 8*

### Large Bag

> 4 cups dehydrated sliced apples, cut into thirds
> ⅔ cup dehydrated cranberries
> 1 cup sugar
> 2 tablespoons cornstarch
> 1 tablespoon apple pie spice

### To Store

Place all ingredients into large bag, seal, and label with cooking instructions.

### Cooking Ingredients

> 6 cups water
> 2 prepared pie crusts
> 1 tablespoon butter, melted
> 1 tablespoon sugar

### Directions

1. Place ingredients from bag into a pot. Add water, stir, bring to a boil, reduce heat to simmer, stir, cover, and simmer for 10 minutes until thickened. Remove from heat and let cool.
2. Preheat oven to 350°F. Roll out prepared pie crusts and cut into quarters.
3. Place ½ cup apple filling into each square, fold, and press into a triangle.
4. Brush each turnover with melted butter and sprinkle with sugar.
5. Place turnovers onto a baking sheet and bake in preheated oven for 50 to 55 minutes or until crust is a golden brown.

# Shredded Zucchini, Coconut, Raisin Oatmeal Cookies

A sweet and unique oatmeal cookie, with a hidden serving of vegetables.

*Makes 2½ dozen*

*Large Bag*

>    1½ cups brown sugar
>    1 cup flour
>    3½ cups rolled oats
>    1 teaspoon salt
>    ½ teaspoon baking soda

*Small Bag*

>    1 cup dehydrated shredded zucchini
>    ½ cup dehydrated shredded coconut
>    1 cup raisins

*To Store*

Place all ingredients into bags. Place small bag into large bag, seal, and label with cooking instructions.

*Cooking Ingredients*

>    3 cups boiling water
>    2 sticks (1 cup) butter, softened
>    1 egg
>    ¼ cup water

*Directions*

1. Place ingredients from small bag into bowl. Add boiling water, cover, and let set while preparing batter.
2. Place ingredients from large bag into a separate mixing bowl. Add butter, egg, and ¼ cup water.
3. Lightly drain extra water from zucchini, coconut, and raisins (do not press or squeeze out water). Stir into batter.
4. Preheat oven to 350°F.
5. Grease a baking pan, and drop 1 tablespoon of batter per cookie onto baking pan.
6. Bake 15 to 18 minutes until golden brown.

# Coconut Macaroons

A rich and tasty treat, and gluten-free!

*Makes 5 dozen*

### Large Bag

    5 cups dehydrated coconut flakes
    ½ teaspoon cream of tartar
    ¼ teaspoon salt
    1⅓ cups sugar

### To Store

Place all ingredients into large bag, seal, and label with cooking instructions.

### Cooking Ingredients

    4 egg whites
    1 teaspoon vanilla extract

### Directions

1. Preheat oven to 325°F. Place ingredients from large bag into mixing bowl. Add egg whites and vanilla, and stir until well blended.
2. Drop 1 tablespoon per cookie onto a greased cookie sheet.
3. Place cookie sheet into preheated oven and bake for 25 minutes or until light golden brown.

# Fruit Bowl Cookies

Fruit salad in a cookie!

*Makes 3 dozen*

*Large Bag*

- 3 cups all-purpose flour
- 1⅓ cup brown sugar
- 1 teaspoon baking soda
- 1 teaspoon baking powder
- ½ teaspoon salt
- ½ teaspoon allspice

*Small Bag*

- 2 tablespoons dehydrated blueberries
- 2 tablespoons dehydrated pineapple tidbits
- 2 tablespoons dehydrated chopped cherries
- ¼ cup dehydrated sliced peaches, cut in thirds
- ¼ cup dehydrated chopped mango
- ½ cup dehydrated coconut flakes
- 2 tablespoons sugar

*To Store*

Place all ingredients into bags. Place small bag into large bag, seal, and label with cooking instructions.

*Cooking Ingredients*

- 1 cup boiling water
- 2 eggs
- 1½ sticks (¾ cup) butter
- 1¼ cup water, divided

*Directions*

1. Place ingredients from small bag into a bowl with boiling water and let set until cool.
2. Preheat oven to 350°F. Place ingredients from large bag into a separate mixing bowl. Add eggs, butter, and ¼ cup water and blend together until a smooth batter. Slowly fold fruit into batter.
3. Drop 1 tablespoon per cookie onto an ungreased cookie sheet.
4. Place into a preheated oven for 15 to 18 minutes or until cookies are golden brown.

# Pineapple, Coconut, and Raisin Oatmeal Cookies

A delicious cookie with a crunch of tropical flavor.

*Makes 2½ dozen*

### Large Bag

> 1½ cups brown sugar
> 1 cup flour
> 3½ cups rolled oats
> 1 teaspoon salt
> ½ teaspoon baking soda

### Small Bag

> ½ cup dehydrated pineapple tidbits
> ½ cup dehydrated shredded coconut
> 1 cup raisins

### To Store

Place all ingredients into bags. Place small bag into large bag, seal, and label with cooking instructions.

### Cooking Ingredients

> 2 cups boiling water
> 2 sticks (1 cup) butter, softened
> 1 egg
> ¼ cup water

### Directions

1. Place ingredients from small bag into a bowl. Add 2 cups boiling water. Let set while preparing batter.
2. Place ingredients from large bag into a separate mixing bowl. Add butter, egg, and ¼ cup water. Mix to a smooth batter.
3. Lightly drain extra water from pineapple, raisins, and coconut (do not press or squeeze out water), then stir the fruit into the batter.
4. Preheat oven to 350°F.
5. Grease a baking pan, and drop 1 tablespoon of batter per cookie onto baking pan.
6. Bake in preheated oven 15 to 18 minutes until golden brown.

# Sweet Potato Pie

Rich. Silky. Heavenly.

*Serves 8*

*Large Bag*

    1 cup dehydrated mashed sweet potatoes, rolled out and cut into squares

*Small Bag*

    ⅓ cup granulated sugar
    ⅓ cup brown sugar
    ½ teaspoon ground ginger
    ½ teaspoon ground cinnamon
    ½ teaspoon ground nutmeg
    ¼ teaspoon allspice

*To Store*

Place all ingredients into bags. Place small bag into large bag, seal, and label with cooking instructions.

*Cooking Ingredients*

    2 cups boiling water
    1 cup milk
    2 eggs
    ¼ cup cooking oil
    1 prepared pie crust

*Directions*

1. Place ingredients from large bag into a pot with boiling water, stir, cover, remove from heat, and let set 15 minutes. Stir until potatoes are hydrated, smooth, and cooled.
2. Preheat oven to 375°F.
3. Place ingredients from small bag into a blender. Add milk, eggs, and oil. Blend until smooth.
4. Add mashed sweet potato from pot to blender, and blend until smooth.
5. Arrange prepared pie crust in a pie pan, and pour sweet potato mixture into pie crust.
6. Place pie in preheated oven and bake 35 to 40 minutes or until golden brown and a knife comes out clean when inserted in middle.

# Chapter 9

# Bread in a Bag

Making homemade bread doesn't require the luxury of time and exceptional effort anymore; not with bread in a bag! Let your home fill with the aroma of these delicate fluffy morsels, effortlessly made with these bread-in-a-bag recipes! Store your recipes in vacuum and Mylar bags, and pull them from storage when you need them.

# Banana Muffins

The mild sweetness of banana is brought to life with honey in these fluffy, moist muffins.

*Makes 12 muffins*

*Large Bag*

> 2¼ cups flour
> ½ cup sugar
> 3 teaspoons baking powder
> ½ teaspoon baking soda
> 1 teaspoon cinnamon
> 1½ tablespoons powdered nonfat milk

*Small Bag*

> 2 cups dehydrated sliced bananas

*To Store*

Place all ingredients into bags. Place small bag into large bag, seal, and label with cooking instructions.

*Cooking Ingredients*

> 2 cups boiling water
> 1 stick (½ cup) butter, softened
> 2 eggs
> ½ cup water
> 2 tablespoons honey

*Directions*

1. Remove 12 banana slices from small bag and set aside for garnish.
2. Place remaining banana slices from small bag in a small bowl. Add 2 cups boiling water to the bowl, cover, and let set until cooled and hydrated. Drain water from bananas.
3. Preheat oven to 350°F. Place ingredients from large bag into blender. Add butter, eggs and ½ cup water. Blend until smooth.
4. Add hydrated bananas to the blender, and blend again until smooth.
5. Line a muffin tin with muffin cups. Pour batter into muffin cups.
6. Place muffins in preheated oven and bake 20 to 25 minutes.
7. Remove muffins from oven and garnish each with 1 slice of dehydrated banana. Drizzle honey over the finished product.

# Raspberry Muffins

The tartness of raspberry is soothed by lemon zest in these aromatic muffins.

*Makes 12*

### Large Bag

    1 cup all-purpose flour
    ¾ cup sugar
    2 teaspoons baking powder

### Small Bag

    1 cup dehydrated raspberries, crushed
    1 teaspoon dehydrated lemon zest

### To Store

Place all ingredients into bags. Place small bag into large bag, seal, and label with cooking instructions.

### Cooking Ingredients

    2 eggs
    1 stick (½ cup) butter, softened
    1 cup water

### Directions

1. Preheat oven to 350°F. Place ingredients from large and small bags in a blender. Add eggs, butter, and water. Blend until smooth.
2. Pour batter into paper muffin cups in muffin tin.
3. Place muffins into preheated oven and bake 20 to 25 minutes.

# Orange Coconut Muffins

These muffins are refreshing without being overly sweet. The perfect summertime muffin.

*Makes 1 dozen*

*Large Bag*

   2 cups all-purpose flour
   1 cup sugar
   1 teaspoon baking soda
   1 teaspoon baking powder
   ½ teaspoon salt

*Small Bag*

   8 dehydrated orange slices, crushed
   ½ cup dehydrated coconut flakes

*To Store*

Place all ingredients into bags. Place small bag into large bag, seal, and label with cooking instructions.

*Cooking Ingredients*

   1 egg
   1 cup sour cream
   ¼ cup cooking oil
   ¼ cup water

*Directions*

1. Place ingredients from large and small bags into a mixing bowl. Add egg, sour cream, cooking oil, and water. Blend until smooth, and let set 5 to 10 minutes.
2. Preheat oven to 350°F.
3. Pour batter into greased muffin tin, then place in preheated oven for 30 to 35 minutes or until golden brown.

# Jalapeño Corn Muffins

Sweet with just the right amount of heat.

*Makes 1 dozen*

### Large Bag

⅔ cup cornmeal
⅔ cup all-purpose flour
1 tablespoon sugar
1½ teaspoons baking powder
1 tablespoon powdered cheese
2 tablespoons crushed dehydrated jalapeño

### To Store

Place all ingredients into large bag, seal, and label with cooking instructions.

### Cooking Ingredients

2 eggs
¼ cup water
2 cups sour cream

### Directions

1. Preheat oven to 350°F.
2. Place ingredients from bag into a mixing bowl. Add eggs, water, and sour cream. Blend together until a smooth batter.
3. Pour batter into a greased muffin tin, and place in preheated oven to bake for 20 minutes or until golden brown.
4. Add sliced jalapeños as a garnish if desired.

# Basil Pesto Biscuits

Don't settle for plain old biscuits; use this unique robust alternative.

*Makes 12 biscuits*

*Large Bag*

>   2½ cups all-purpose flour
>   2 teaspoons baking powder
>   ¾ teaspoon salt
>   3 tablespoons powdered nonfat milk

*Small Bag*

>   ⅓ cup dehydrated sun-dried tomatoes, cut into small pieces
>   2 tablespoons Basil Pesto Seasoning (see page 18)

*To Store*

Place all ingredients into bags. Place small bag into large bag, seal, and label with cooking instructions.

*Cooking Ingredients*

>   1 egg
>   ¾ cup water
>   1 cup olive oil
>   1 cup grated Parmesan cheese

*Directions*

1.  Preheat oven to 350ºF. Pour ingredients from large and small bags into a bowl.
2.  In a separate bowl, add egg, water, and oil and whisk together. Pour liquid mixture into dry ingredients along with the Parmesan cheese, stirring until all ingredients are moist.
3.  Using a ¼-cup measuring spoon, scoop batter onto a nonstick baking pan: 1 scoop per biscuit.
4.  Bake biscuits in preheated oven for approximately 20 to 25 minutes or until tops are golden brown.

# Cranberry-Peach Cornbread

Fragrant and fruity cornbread recipe in a snap.

*Serves 9*

### Large Bag

> 1 cup cornmeal
> ¾ cup all-purpose flour
> 2 tablespoons sugar
> 1½ teaspoons baking powder
> ½ teaspoon baking soda
> 1 cup powdered milk

### Small Bag

> ½ cup dehydrated cranberries
> ½ cup dehydrated chopped peaches

### To Store

Place all ingredients into bags. Place small bag into large bag, seal, and label with cooking instructions.

### Cooking Ingredients

> 2½ cups lukewarm water
> ¼ cup oil
> 2 eggs

### Directions

1. Preheat oven to 350°F.
2. Place all ingredients from large and small bags into a mixing bowl. Add water, oil, and eggs. Mix all ingredients until batter is smooth.
3. Grease an 8 x 10-inch pan, and pour batter into pan. Bake in preheated oven for 35 minutes or until a knife comes out clean when inserted in center and top is golden brown.

# Tomato and Herb Scones

These hearty melt-in-your-mouth scones have a robust flavor.

*Makes 8*

*Large Bag*

> 2 cups all-purpose flour
> 1½ teaspoons baking powder
> ¼ teaspoon salt

*Small Bag*

> ½ cup crumbled dehydrated tomato slices
> 1 tablespoon crumbled dehydrated basil

*To Store*

Place all ingredients into bags. Place small bag into large bag, seal, and label with cooking instructions.

*Cooking Ingredients*

> ½ stick (¼ cup) butter
> 2 egg whites
> ¾ cup milk
> 1 tablespoon olive oil

*Directions*

1. Preheat oven to 375°F.
2. Place ingredients from large and small bags into a mixing bowl. Add butter, egg whites, and milk, and blend together until a large dough ball forms.
3. Press dough into an 8-inch circle, score into 8 pieces, place on greased baking sheet, and drizzle olive oil over the top.
4. Place pan into preheated oven and bake 25 minutes or until golden brown.

# Orange-Poppy Seed Quick Bread

The subtle sweetness of orange with the earthiness of poppy seed, in a fragrant and fluffy loaf.

*Makes 1 medium loaf*

### Large Bag

> 2 cups flour
>
> 1 cup sugar
>
> 3 tablespoons nonfat powdered milk
>
> 2 teaspoons baking powder
>
> ½ teaspoon salt
>
> 1 tablespoon poppy seeds

### Small Bag

> 8 dehydrated orange slices with peel, crushed
>
> 2 tablespoons sugar

### To Store

Place all ingredients into bags. Place small bag into large bag, seal, and label with cooking instructions.

### Cooking Ingredients

> 1½ cups water
>
> 2 eggs
>
> ¼ cup cooking oil

### Directions

1. Preheat oven to 350°F.
2. Place ingredients from large and small bags into mixing bowl. Add water, eggs, and oil. Mix all ingredients until a smooth batter.
3. Pour batter into a greased bread loaf pan and place into preheated oven to bake for 45 to 50 minutes, or until top is golden brown and knife comes out clean when inserted in the middle.

# Cheese and Hot Pepper Bread

A satisfying zesty loaf with a lasting mild heat. Great for watching the game.

*Makes 1 loaf*

*Large Bag*

> 2½ cups all-purpose flour
> 1 tablespoon sugar
> 1½ teaspoons baking powder
> ½ teaspoon baking soda
> 3 tablespoons nonfat powdered milk
> 1 teaspoon salt
> ¼ cup powdered cheese
> 1 tablespoon crushed dehydrated hot chile peppers

*To Store*

Place all ingredients into large bag, seal, and label with cooking instructions.

*Cooking Ingredients*

> ½ cup cooking oil
> 1 cup milk
> 2 eggs

*Directions*

1. Preheat oven to 350°F.
2. Place ingredients from bag into a mixing bowl. Add oil, milk, and eggs. Blend until smooth.
3. Pour into a greased bread loaf pan. Place into preheated oven and bake for 50 to 55 minutes.

# Apricot-Cranberry-Banana Bread

Quick and easy. Sweet and silky. Ready in no time. A perfect side portion.

*Makes 1 mini loaf*

### Large Bag

   1 cup flour
   ½ cup brown sugar
   ½ teaspoon salt
   1 teaspoon baking powder

### Small Bag

   ¼ cup dehydrated sliced banana, broken into small bits
   2 tablespoons chopped dehydrated apricots
   2 tablespoons dehydrated cranberries

### To Store

Place all ingredients into bags. Place small bag into large bag, seal, and label with cooking instructions.

### Cooking Ingredients

   1 egg
   ¼ cup cooking oil
   ½ cup water

### Directions

1. Preheat oven to 350°F.
2. Place ingredients from large and small bags into a mixing bowl. Add egg, oil, and water. Blend until smooth, and let set 15 minutes.
3. Pour batter into a greased mini bread loaf pan. Place into preheated oven and bake 35 to 40 minutes.

# Zucchini-Pineapple-Coconut Bread

A delightful light bread with bright tropical flavors.

*Makes 2 loaves*

*Large Bag*

> 4 cups flour
> 3 cups sugar
> 2½ teaspoons baking powder
> 1 teaspoon baking soda
> 1 teaspoon salt

*Medium Bag*

> 3 cups dehydrated shredded zucchini
> ½ cup dehydrated crushed pineapple
> ½ cup dehydrated shredded coconut

*To Store*

Place all ingredients into bags. Place medium bag into large bag, seal, and label with cooking instructions.

*Cooking Ingredients*

> 4 cups boiling water
> 1½ cups cooking oil
> 4 eggs
> ½ cup water

*Directions*

1. Place ingredients from medium bag into a bowl. Add boiling water. Let set until cool and hydrated. Drain water (do not press or squeeze).
2. Preheat oven to 350°F.
3. Place ingredients from large bag into a blender. Add oil, eggs, and water. Blend until a smooth batter, then stir in hydrated zucchini, coconut, and pineapple until well blended.
4. Pour batter into a greased bread loaf pan. Place pan into preheated oven and bake 50 to 55 minutes.

# Olive and Oregano Quick Bread

Fragrant and full of flavor; perfect to use with many different appetizers.

*Makes 1 loaf*

### Large Bag

- 2 cups all-purpose flour
- 1 teaspoon baking soda
- 1 teaspoon baking powder
- ¼ teaspoon salt
- 1 tablespoon powdered cheese
- 3 tablespoons powdered nonfat milk

### Small Bag

- ¼ cup dehydrated sliced green olives
- ¼ cup dehydrated sliced black olives
- 1 tablespoon crushed dehydrated oregano

### To Store

Place all ingredients into bags. Place small bag into large bag, seal, and label with cooking instructions.

### Cooking Ingredients

- ½ cup olive oil
- 1 egg
- 1 cup water

### Directions

1. Place ingredients from large and small bags into a mixing bowl. Add olive oil, egg, and water, blend until a smooth batter, and let set for 10 minutes.
2. Preheat oven to 350°F.
3. Pour batter into a greased 9 x 5-inch bread loaf pan, then place into preheated oven and bake for 35 to 40 minutes or until golden brown.

# Pumpkin-Banana Bread

Sweet and moist, an instant autumn classic.

*Makes 2 loaves*

*Large Bag*

> 3½ cups flour
> 2 cups sugar
> 1 teaspoon baking powder
> 2 teaspoons baking soda
> 1½ teaspoons salt
> 1 teaspoon ground ginger
> ¼ teaspoon nutmeg
> 1 teaspoon cinnamon

*Small Bag*

> ¼ cup powdered dehydrated pumpkin
> ½ cup dehydrated banana slices

*To Store*

Place all ingredients into bags. Place small bag into large bag, seal, and label with cooking instructions.

*Cooking Ingredients*

> 2 cups boiling water
> 4 eggs
> 1 cup cooking oil
> 1 cup water

*Directions*

1. Place ingredients from small bag into a bowl with boiling water. Let sit until cool and thickened. Place into a blender and blend until smooth.
2. Preheat oven to 350°F.
3. Place ingredients from large bag into a mixing bowl. Add eggs, oil, and 1 cup of water. Blend until a smooth batter.
4. Fold the cooled puréed pumpkin and banana into batter until well blended and smooth.
5. Pour batter into 2 well-greased 9 x 5-inch bread pans and place inside preheated oven to bake for 55 minutes or until golden brown and a knife comes out clean when inserted in middle.

# Chapter 10

# Breakfast in a Bag

Morning is often the most stressful time of the day! You and your significant other are rushing to make it to work, half of the kids are careening recklessly through the halls getting ready for school, while the other half are still asleep. You glance at your watch, sigh loudly, and settle for a toaster pastry or a granola bar. Don't sacrifice breakfast! It is, after all, the most important meal of the day! Let us help you make this portrait a thing of the past. With easy "breakfast in a bag" recipes, breakfast will be the least of your morning worries. Now for goodness sake, has anyone seen Kaitlyn's left ballet slipper?

# Mint Blueberry Shake

This easy-to-make shake is packed with antioxidants and is a great way to start your day.

*Serves 2*

*Medium Bag*

>    1 cup dehydrated kale
>    1 cup dehydrated spinach
>    ¼ cup dehydrated blueberries
>    3 dehydrated mint leaves
>    3 tablespoons dehydrated sliced strawberries

*To Store*

Place all ingredients into a blender and grind to powder. Place powder into a medium bag, seal, and label with preparation instructions (4 medium bags can fit into 1 large Mylar bag).

*Wet Ingredients*

>    2 cups water
>    1½ cups coconut water
>    ½ cup ice

*Directions*

Pour contents of bag into a blender with the wet ingredients. Blend, serve, enjoy.

# Tropical Shake

A refreshing blast of tropical flavor to invigorate the morning.

*Serves 2*

### Medium Bag

> ¼ cup dehydrated pineapple tidbits
> 12 dehydrated banana slices
> ¼ cup dehydrated parsley
> 1 teaspoon coarsely ground dehydrated ginger
> ¼ teaspoon dehydrated lime zest

### To Store

Place all ingredients into a blender and grind to powder. Place powder into a medium bag, seal, and label with preparation instructions (4 medium bags can fit into 1 large Mylar bag).

### Wet Ingredients

> 2 cups water
> ½ cup probiotic coconut water
> ½ cup vanilla Greek yogurt
> ½ cup ice

### Directions

Pour contents of bag into a blender with the wet ingredients. Blend, serve, enjoy.

# Banana-Peanut Butter Protein Bars

These bars are high in protein and desirable oils such as oleic acid, making it a healthy choice to get you moving. About 12 grams of protein per bar. For an additional protein boost, replace a scoop of the powdered peanut butter with a scoop of your favorite protein powder.

*Makes 10 bars*

### Large Bag

> 1 cup rolled old-fashioned oats
> 1 cup quick-cooking oats

### Medium Bag

> ⅔ cup raisins
> 1 cup dehydrated banana slices, chopped in blender
> ¼ cup sunflower seeds

### Small Bag

> ¼ cup powdered peanut butter
> ½ teaspoon salt
> ¼ cup flaxseed

### To Store

Place all ingredients into bags. Place smaller bags into large bag, seal, and label with cooking instructions.

### Cooking Ingredients

> 1½ cups warm water
> ¼ cup coconut oil
> 2 eggs
> ¼ cup honey

### Directions

1. Place ingredients from large, medium, and small bags into a large mixing bowl. Add water, coconut oil, eggs, and honey. Fold all ingredients together until blended.
2. Preheat oven to 350°F.
3. Grease an 8 x 10-inch baking pan, then press and flatten batter into pan.
4. Place pan into preheated oven and bake 20 to 25 minutes or until lightly brown. Let cool. Cut into 2 x 4-inch bars.

# Fruit Strata

Perfect for an easy and refreshing family breakfast.

*Serves 8*

### Large Bag

2¼ cups dehydrated apple slices
2¼ cups dehydrated sliced peaches
½ cup dehydrated pineapple tidbits
1 cup raisins
½ cup dehydrated shredded coconut

### Medium Bag

4 cups dehydrated bread cubes
1 cup brown sugar

### To Store

Place all ingredients into bags. Place medium bag into large bag, seal, and label with cooking instructions.

### Cooking Ingredients

8 cups boiling water
8 eggs
8 ounces cream cheese
½ cup half-and-half

### Directions

1. Place ingredients from large bag into a mixing bowl. Add boiling water, cover, and let set 10 to 15 minutes until water is lukewarm. Drain.
2. Preheat oven to 325°F.
3. Add ingredients from medium bag to the hydrated fruit, gently toss together, and place into a generously greased 10- to 12-inch square deep-dish pan.
4. In a separate bowl, beat eggs, cream cheese, and half-and-half until smooth. Pour over the bread cubes and fruit.
5. Place pan in preheated oven for 1 hour or until it puffs up and turns golden brown.

# Spinach and Dill Potato Pancakes

A satisfying morning dish with a warm soft inside, aromatic flavors of dill and spinach, and a gentle outer crunch. Try with a dollop of sour cream or applesauce.

*Makes 10 pancakes*

### Large Bag

> 4 cups dehydrated shredded potatoes
> 1 cup dehydrated shredded onion

### Small Bag

> ½ cup all-purpose flour
> 1 tablespoon Spinach & Dill Seasoning (see page 20)

### To Store

Place all ingredients into bags. Place small bag into large bag, seal, and label with cooking instructions.

### Cooking Ingredients

> 5 cups boiling water
> 2 eggs
> 2 tablespoons olive oil
> Sour cream or applesauce (optional)

### Directions

1. Place ingredients from large bag into a mixing bowl. Add boiling water, cover, and let cool.
2. Drain off excess water, then place ingredients from small bag into the bowl and stir until blended.
3. Add eggs and continue to stir until blended.
4. Heat olive oil in a skillet over medium high heat until hot.
5. Place ½ cup batter per potato pancake into the skillet. Cook each side until a crispy golden brown.
6. Serve hot with a dollop of sour cream or applesauce, if desired.

# Breakfast Bake

Just add water for an easy breakfast casserole your family is sure to love.

*Serves 6*

### Large Bag

> 4 cups dehydrated shredded potatoes (hash browns)
> ¼ cup dehydrated chopped onions
> 2 tablespoons dehydrated chopped red bell pepper
> 1 cup dehydrated baby spinach

### Small Bag

> ½ cup powdered egg
> 3 tablespoons nonfat powdered milk
> ¼ cup powdered cheese

### To Store

Place all ingredients into bags. Place small bag into large bag, seal, and label with cooking instructions.

### Cooking Ingredients

> 6 cups warm water

### Directions

1. Preheat oven to 350°F.
2. Place ingredients from small bag into a blender with warm water. Blend until smooth.
3. Place ingredients from large bag into a 10 x 10-inch greased oven-safe pan.
4. Pour contents of blender over ingredients in pan, then place pan into preheated oven for 35 minutes or until golden brown.

# Ham and Spinach Hash Brown Bake

A simple and hearty breakfast casserole.

*Serves 6*

*Large Bag*

> 4 cups dehydrated shredded potatoes (hash browns)
> 2½ cups dehydrated baby spinach
> ½ cup dehydrated shredded onion
> 1 cup dehydrated thinly sliced tomatoes

*Small Bag*

> 2 teaspoons crushed basil
> 1 cup all-purpose flour
> 2 teaspoons baking powder
> ½ teaspoons salt
> 3 tablespoons nonfat powdered milk

*To Store*

Place all ingredients into bags. Place small bag into large bag, seal, and label with cooking instructions.

*Cooking Ingredients*

> 6 cups boiling water
> 1 tablespoon olive oil
> 2 cups cubed cooked ham
> 1 cup water
> 8 eggs

*Directions*

1. Place ingredients from large bag into a bowl. Add boiling water and let set 10 to 15 minutes. Lightly drain (do not squeeze water out). Add 1 tablespoon olive oil and stir.
2. Preheat oven to 350°F.
3. Spread vegetable mixture evenly into the bottom of a 9 x 13-inch baking dish.
4. Sprinkle ham over the top of spinach and tomato mixture.
5. Place ingredients from small bag into a mixing bowl. Add water and eggs and blend until smooth.
6. Pour egg mixture over top of ham, spinach, and tomato mixture.
7. Place baking dish into preheated oven and bake 30 to 35 minutes.

# Hash Brown-Spinach-Cheese Bake

This breakfast casserole pairs hearty hash browns with savory spinach.

*Serves 6*

### Large Bag

> 5 cups dehydrated shredded potatoes (hash browns)
> 1 cup dehydrated shredded onions
> 1 cup dehydrated spinach

### Small Bag

> ½ cup powdered cheese
> ½ cup powdered nonfat milk
> 1 tablespoon flour

### To Store

Place all ingredients into bags. Place small bag into large bag, seal, and label with cooking instructions.

### Cooking Ingredients

> 8 cups warm water
> ½ stick (¼ cup) butter, softened

### Directions

1. Preheat oven to 350°F.
2. In a greased Dutch oven, mix ingredients from large and small bags together with water and butter.
3. Cover and place in preheated oven for 30 minutes. Remove cover, and place back in oven for an additional 15 minutes or until top is golden brown.

# Spicy Sausage Breakfast Bake

Spice up your morning with this easy breakfast casserole.

*Serves 6*

*Large Bag*

    3 cups dehydrated shredded potatoes
    1 cup dehydrated sliced tomatoes
    ½ cup dehydrated shredded onions
    1 tablespoon dehydrated chopped jalapeños

*Cooking Ingredients*

    6 cups boiling water
    6 large eggs
    ½ cup half & half
    2 cups cooked and drained crumbled sausage
    2 cups mozzarella cheese

*Directions*

1. Preheat to 350 degrees F.
2. Place ingredients from large bag into a bowl and add water. Cover and let set 15 minutes. Drain any remaining water.
3. In another large bowl beat eggs and half & half together. Stir in sausage and rehydrated ingredients.
4. Pour all contents into a 10 x 10-inch greased baking pan. Sprinkle cheese on top.
5. Place into preheated oven and bake for 35 minutes or until the top is golden brown and cheese is melted.

## PREPACKAGED VARIETY PACK OATMEAL

Did you ever purchase instant oatmeal and wish it had more fruit? Well, you no longer have to say "Where's the fruit?"

Place each serving into its own small bag and store in a larger bag along with a variety of other flavors.

If you're backpacking, just add 1 cup of boiling water to the oatmeal, cover, and let set for 3–5 minutes.

# Apples and Cinnamon

*Serves 1*

### Small Bag

> ½ cup instant oats
> ½ teaspoon sugar
> ½ teaspoon cinnamon
> 3 tablespoons dehydrated sliced apples, quartered

### Cooking Ingredients

> 1 cup hot water

### Directions

Combine ingredients from small bag with hot water in a microwave-safe bowl. Microwave 1 minute on high. Let set 1 to 2 minutes.

# Peaches and Brown Sugar

*Serves 1*

*Small Bag*

½ cup instant oats
2 teaspoons brown sugar
3 tablespoons dehydrated sliced peaches, quartered

*Cooking Ingredients*

1 cup hot water

*Directions*

Combine ingredients from small bag with hot water in a microwave-safe bowl. Microwave 1 minute on high. Let set 1 to 2 minutes.

# Apple-Peach-Raisin

*Serves 1*

*Small Bag*

½ cup instant oats
2 teaspoons brown sugar
1 tablespoon dehydrated sliced peaches, quartered
1 tablespoon dehydrated sliced apples, quartered
1 tablespoon raisins

*Cooking Ingredients*

1 cup hot water

*Directions*

Combine ingredients from small bag with hot water in a microwave-safe bowl. Microwave 1 minute on high. Let set 1 to 2 minutes.

# Banana-Walnut

*Serves 1*

### Small Bag

- ½ cup instant oats
- 2 teaspoons brown sugar
- 3 tablespoons dehydrated sliced bananas, halved
- 1 tablespoon walnuts

### Cooking Ingredients

- 1 cup hot water

### Directions

Combine ingredients from small bag with hot water in a microwave-safe bowl. Microwave 1 minute on high. Let set 1 to 2 minutes.

# Raspberry-Blueberry Swirl

*Serves 1*

### Small Bag

- ½ cup instant oats
- 2 teaspoons sugar
- 2 dehydrated raspberries, crushed
- 1 tablespoon dehydrated blueberries

### Cooking Ingredients

- 1 cup hot water

### Directions

Combine ingredients from small bag with hot water in a microwave-safe bowl. Microwave 1 minute on high. Let set 1 to 2 minutes.

# Coconut-Pineapple-Raisin

*Serves 1*

*Small Bag*

> ½ cup instant oats
> 1 tablespoon dehydrated crushed pineapple
> 1 tablespoon dehydrated coconut flakes, crushed
> 1 tablespoon raisins

*Cooking Ingredients*

> 1 cup hot water

*Directions*

Combine ingredients from small bag with hot water in a microwave-safe bowl. Microwave 1 minute on high. Let set 1 to 2 minutes.

# Blueberry Syrup

Your favorite fruit can be used to spruce up pancakes, ice cream, cheesecake, and so much more.

*Makes about 2 cups*

*Medium Bag*

> 1 cup dehydrated blueberries
> ½ cup granulated sugar

*Cooking Ingredients*

> 3 cups water

## Fun Tip

Substitute 1 cup chopped dehydrated apricots for a delicious alternative.

*Directions*

1. Place ingredients from medium bag into a saucepan and add water.
2. Bring to a boil, reduce to simmer, stirring occasionally for 20–30 minutes until thickened.
3. Serve hot or place in the refrigerator to chill. Leftover syrup must be refrigerated.

# Chapter 11

# Backpacker Meals and Snacks

T his chapter is geared toward the adventurers, hikers, mountaineers, cartographers, and backpackers of the world! A true wanderlust-filled voyager knows you bring with you only lightweight necessities that are easy to carry.

The majority of the weight in most foods is water. Luckily for you, you have us—the experts in food dehydration! When you dehydrate foods, they not only store for longer, but they become significantly more compact and lightweight. In this chapter you will find easy-to-carry snacks and single servings that only require the addition of hot water. You can pour hot water directly into the bag and fold or clamp it shut. After a short wait, your meal is rehydrated and ready to eat straight from the bag. This will leave you with more time to explore and less weight on your back!

# Kale Protein Shake

This easy-to-make shake can be poured right into your water bottle to give you that extra boost of energy that you will need on the trail.

*Serves 1*

*Small Bag*

>  1 scoop vanilla protein powder
>  1 cup dehydrated kale
>  2 dehydrated orange slices with peels
>  1 teaspoon coarsely ground dehydrated ginger

*To Store*

Place all ingredients into a blender and grind to powder. Place powder into a small bag, seal, and label with preparation instructions.

*Wet Ingredients*

>  2 cups water

*Directions*

When ready to use, pour the contents of the bag into 2 cups water and shake until powder is dissolved. Drink and enjoy.

# Matcha Pear Protein Shake

Matcha is a powdered green tea. Simply pour right into your water bottle and go!

*Serves 1*

### Small Bag

>    1 scoop vanilla protein powder
>    1 cup dehydrated spinach
>    ¼ cup dehydrated chopped pears
>    ½ teaspoon matcha tea powder
>    ⅓ cup nonfat milk powder

### To Store

Place all ingredients into a blender and grind to powder. Place powder into a small bag, seal, and label with preparation instructions.

### Wet Ingredients

>    2 cups water

### Directions

When ready to use, pour the contents of the bag into 2 cups water and shake until powder is dissolved. Drink and enjoy.

# Carrot Crackers

Easy to make and an easy snack while out on the trail.

*Makes 2 dozen*

### Ingredients

>    4 cups cooked (al dente) sliced carrots
>    ½ cup coconut, raw or flaked
>    ½ cup flaxseeds
>    2 tablespoons chia seeds
>    ½ cup sunflower seeds

*Directions*

1. Place ingredients into a blender. Puree until smooth, then pour onto dehydrator drying tray.
2. Square off with spatula.
3. Dehydrate at 125°F for 4 hours. The mixture will still be soft.
4. Cut the mixture into bite-size squares and place back into the dehydrator for another 4 to 5 hours.
5. Seal and store in small bags.

# Flaxseed Crackers

Try any of our spices from the Seasonings chapter (see page 15) to make a variety of flavored crackers. A delicious crunch at any altitude!

*Makes about 2 dozen crackers*

*Ingredients*

   2 cups ground flaxseeds
   1 cup whole flaxseeds
   1½ cups sunflower seeds
   ¼ cup chia seeds
   ¼ cup sesame seeds
   1 teaspoon Citrus & Dill spice (see page 16)
   3½ cups warm water

*Directions*

1. Place all dry ingredients into a large bowl. Add warm water, stir, cover, and let set 15 minutes.
2. Pour the mixture onto dehydrator dryer sheet. Square it off with a rubber spatula, spreading it about a quarter-inch thick.
3. Dehydrate at 125°F for 3 to 4 hours. The mixture will still be somewhat soft. Cut mixture into 2 x 2-inch squares.
4. Place back in dehydrator for another 4 to 5 hours.
5. Seal and store in small bags.

# Spicy Bean Burrito

Just add water and share spicy burritos around the campfire.

*Serves 1*

### Large Bag

    1 large flour burrito wrap

### Small Bag

    ¼ cup dehydrated refried beans
    3 dehydrated tomato slices, crumbled
    10 dehydrated baby spinach leaves
    ½ teaspoon Taco Seasoning (see page 16)
    1 teaspoon powdered cheese

### To Store

Place all ingredients into bags. Place small bag into large bag, seal, and label with cooking instructions.

### Cooking Ingredients

    ⅔ cup boiling water

### Directions

1. Remove whole-wheat burrito wrap from large Mylar bag and set aside.
2. Open the small bag and pour contents into large bag.
3. Add boiling water, clamp shut, and let set 15 minutes.
4. Open bag, stir ingredients until smooth, and spoon on burrito wrap.

# Tuna Hawaiian Stew

Quick and easy stew in 15 minutes. Less time for meal prep = more time for campfire stories.

*Serves 1*

*Large Bag*

> 2 tablespoons dehydrated pineapple tidbits
> 1 tablespoon dehydrated peas
> ½ cup dehydrated shredded potatoes
> 1 tablespoon dehydrated diced onions
> 1 teaspoon dehydrated coconut flakes
> 3 tablespoons powdered nonfat milk
> 1 tablespoon all-purpose flour
> ½ teaspoon Citrus & Dill Seasoning (see page 16)

*To Store*

Place all ingredients into large bag, seal, and label with cooking instructions.

*Cooking Ingredients*

> 2½ cups water
> 1 (2.6-ounce) pouch tuna in water

*Directions*

1. Add ingredients from bag to a pot.
2. Add water, stir, bring to boil, and stir until thickened.
3. Fold in tuna, cover, and let set 15 minutes.

# Cheesy Mushroom Couscous

This dish can be made right in the bag; just add water!

*Serves 1*

### Large Bag

- ½ cup uncooked couscous
- 2 tablespoons dehydrated sliced mushrooms
- 2 teaspoons powdered cheese
- 2 teaspoons powdered nonfat milk

### To Store

Place all ingredients into large bag, seal, and label with cooking instructions.

### Cooking Ingredients

- ⅔ cup boiling water

### Directions

1. Open large Mylar bag.
2. Add boiling water, stir, clamp bag shut, and let set for 25 minutes.

# Potato, Apple, Veggie Pancake

Crunchy tasty treat with a serving of fruit and vegetables.

*Serves 1*

### Large Bag

- 1 cup dehydrated shredded potatoes
- ¼ cup dehydrated chopped sliced apples
- ¼ cup dehydrated baby spinach
- 1 tablespoon dehydrated diced onions
- 3 tablespoons powdered eggs
- ¼ cup all-purpose flour

### To Store

Place all ingredients into large bag, seal, and label with cooking instructions.

*Cooking Ingredients*

  2 cups warm water

*Directions*

1. Open large Mylar bag.
2. Add warm water, clamp bag shut, shake bag vigorously, and let set for 20 minutes.
3. Shake bag again, then pour contents into a hot, greased skillet. Cook both sides until golden brown.

# Spiced Dehydrated Veggie Trail Mix

These dehydrated and seasoned veggies are delicious as a unique trail mix, on or off the trail. For an extra flavor boost, sprinkle the veggies with soy sauce before dehydrating.

*Serves 1*

*Medium Bag*

  ½ cup dehydrated halved cherry tomatoes
  ½ cup dehydrated halved Brussels sprouts
  1 handful dehydrated kale
  1 teaspoon Sweet Asian Spice (see page 24)

*Directions*

Combine all ingredients in a medium bag and shake to coat. Open and enjoy.

# Veggie Omelette

A fluffy morning treat with no effort, giving you more time to enjoy the sunrise.

*Serves 1*

### Large Bag

> 3 tablespoons powdered eggs
> 1 teaspoon crushed dehydrated tomato slices
> 1 teaspoon dehydrated diced onion
> 1 teaspoon crushed dehydrated kale
> ½ teaspoon Citrus & Dill Seasoning (see page 16)

### To Store

Place all ingredients into large bag, seal, and label with cooking instructions.

### Cooking Ingredients

> ½ cup warm water

### Directions

1. Open bag, and pour contents into a plastic travel cup with lid.
2. Add ½ cup warm water, replace the lid, and shake vigorously for 2 minutes. Set aside for a few minutes while your greased skillet heats up.
3. Pour egg mixture into hot skillet. Cook both sides until firm, 2 to 3 minutes.

# Italian Pasta

Just add water for pasta that you can make right in the bag.

*Serves 1*

Cook pasta before dehydrating for instant backpacker pasta.
1 cup angel hair spaghetti, cooked, twirled into a bird's nest,
Place on the dehydrator, at 125°F for 10 to 12 hours

*Large Bag*

> 1 angel hair pasta bird's nest
> 1 teaspoon dehydrated sliced black olives
> 1 tablespoon dehydrated sliced mushrooms
> ½ teaspoon Italian Seasoning (see page 19)
> ½ teaspoon powdered dehydrated tomato paste

*To Store*

Place all ingredients into large bag, seal, and label with cooking instructions.

*Cooking Ingredients*

> 1¼ cups boiling water

*Directions*

1. Open Mylar bag.
2. Add 1¼ cups boiling water, clamp bag shut, and let set 10 to 15 minutes.
3. Open bag, stir, and enjoy.

# Squash and Apple Rollup

Easy to eat while on the move, and tastes delicious too.

*Makes 6*

*Ingredients*

    1½ cups puréed squash
    1½ cup applesauce
    ½ teaspoon cinnamon

*Directions*

1. Place all ingredients into a blender, and purée until smooth.
2. Pour ½-cup circles of mixture onto a dehydrator dryer sheet.
3. Dehydrate at 125°F for 12 hours until dry and flexible.
4. Roll up circles and store in a sealed bag.

# Wasabi, Kale, Sesame Seed, Rice Rollups

The right amount of heat and crunch, in a travel friendly package.

*Makes 6*

*Cooking Ingredients*

    2 cups cooked white rice
    ¾ cups water
    2 tablespoons soy sauce
    1 tablespoon wasabi
    2 cups chopped and packed kale
    4 tablespoons sesame seeds

*Directions*

1. Place rice, water, soy sauce, and wasabi into a blender.
2. Purée until smooth, and place into a mixing bowl.
3. Bring a pot of water to a boil. Blanch chopped kale in boiling water for 30 seconds or less, then drain water.
4. Fold kale and sesame seeds into mixing bowl with rice mixture.

5. Pour ½-cup circles of mixture onto a dehydrator dryer sheet until all is used.
6. Dehydrate at 125°F for 12 hours (after 8 hours flip over to other side). Should be dry and flexible.
7. Roll up the circles and store in sealed bags.

# Roasted Red Pepper-Tomato Soup

A velvety and zesty hot soup, ready in a flash.

*Serves 1*

*Small Bag*

> 1 tablespoon Spicy Roasted Red Pepper Seasoning (see page 17)
> 1 teaspoon powdered dehydrated tomato paste
> ¼ teaspoon powdered dehydrated chiles

*To Store*

Place all ingredients into small bag, seal, and label with cooking instructions.

*Cooking Ingredients*

> 1½ cups boiling water

*Directions*

Pour contents of small bag and boiling water into a bowl, stir, and let set 2 minutes.

# Apple-Raisin Dessert

The perfect on-the-go sugary and spiced snack.

*Serves 1*

### Large Bag

> 1 cup dehydrated sliced apples
> ¼ cup raisins
> 1 tablespoon brown sugar
> 1 teaspoon cornstarch
> ½ teaspoon apple pie spice

### To Store

Place all ingredients into large bag, seal, and label with cooking instructions.

### Cooking Ingredients

> 1¼ cups boiling water

### Directions

1. Open large Mylar bag.
2. Add boiling water, stir, clamp bag shut, and let set 15 minutes.
3. Open bag, stir, and enjoy.

# Fruit Delight

Coconut-coated springtime flavors in a bag; ready for sightseeing.

*Serves 1*

### Large Bag

¼ cup dehydrated sliced peaches, halved

¼ cup dehydrated orange slices (without the peels)

1 tablespoon dehydrated coconut flakes

8 dehydrated banana slices

1 tablespoon raisins

### To Store

Place all ingredients into large bag, seal, and label with cooking instructions.

### Cooking Ingredients

1¼ cups boiling water

### Directions

1. Open Mylar bag.
2. Add boiling water, clamp bag shut, and let set 25 to 30 minutes until cooled and hydrated.
3. Enjoy.

# Outro

Thank you all for reading along with us as we dove deep into the exploration of many fun food dehydration and storage marvels. We walked you through the basics of meal storage, taught you about our pour-and-go slow-cooker meals, and gave you a vibrant cornucopia of meals, desserts, and snacks in a bag! We hope you have learned and laughed with us, and tasted many new things. Further, we hope this book has changed the way you prepare food for yourself and your family, to put more money back in your pocket and more free time on your calendar. Oh! Soup's ready!

—Your Guides, Tammy, Steve, and September

# Index